THE HISTORY OF
NEW
ENGLAND

CANDACE FLOYD

Text and captions: Candace Floyd
Design: Design Box
Editorial: Martin Bramwell and Pauline Graham
Commissioning Editor: Andrew Preston
Photographic Research: Leora Kahn
Production: Ruth Arthur, Sally Connolly, David Proffit, Andrew Whitelaw
Director of Publishing: David Gibbon
Director of Production: Gerald Hughes

**Illustrations by UPI/Bettmann Archives
and National Archives, Washington, D.C.**

CLB 2326
© 1990 Colour Library Books Ltd, Godalming, Surrey, England.
All rights reserved.
This 1990 edition published by Portland House,
distributed by Outlet Book Company, Inc, a Random House Company,
225 Park Avenue South, New York, New York 10003.
Colour separations by Advance Laser Graphic Arts (International) Ltd, Hong Kong.
Printed and bound in Italy.
ISBN 0 517 68906 5
8 7 6 5 4 3 2 1

Acknowledgements:

Quotations from *A Little Commonwealth: Family Life in Plymouth Colony* by John Demos, © 1970,
reproduced by kind permission of Oxford University Press.

Quotations from *The Ideological Origins of the American Revolution* by Bernard Bailyn. © 1967; and *The
Complete Works of Ralph Waldo Emerson*, © 1971, by kind permission of the President and Fellows of
Harvard University College.

THE HISTORY OF
NEW ENGLAND

CANDACE FLOYD

PORTLAND HOUSE

CONTENTS

AN ABUNDANT LAND   7

1   TURBULENT BEGINNINGS   11

2   INDEPENDENCE!   69

3   STATEHOOD AND THE NEW ENGLAND FEDERALISTS   117

4   A NEW WORKPLACE AND THE AGE OF REFORM   147

5   ABOLITION, CIVIL WAR, AND WOMEN'S RIGHTS   177

6   THE CHANGING NEW ENGLANDER   223

7   NEW ENGLANDERS AT WORK   243

8   DEMOCRATIC VICTORY   259

9   CHANGING ATTITUDES, NEW ECONOMIES   269

AN ABUNDANT LAND

Upon their arrival, the Pilgrims were greeted by Massasoit, the Chief of the Wampanoags. The Pilgrims and the tribe signed a peace treaty that lasted for more than fifty years, until King Philip's War in 1675. By then, the peacekeepers for the two peoples – Governor William Bradford and Massasoit – were dead and the fighting that ensued forced many settlers temporarily from their homesteads and speeded the end of the Indian way of life in New England. Facing page: an engraving of the two peacekeepers published by Lippincott, Grambo & Company, Philadelphia. Overleaf background: a plan of the Battle of Lake George, New York, which took place in 1755 during the French and Indian War.

When the first English colonists arrived in New England, they found a land inhabited by nearly 100,000 native Americans. Here, on the rugged shorelines and in the wooded interiors, two cultures and two ways of using land collided. From glacial tundra more than 12,000 years ago, to modern age forests beginning 7,000 years ago, and on into agricultural and later industrial landscapes, the land that is New England has shaped the character of the peoples inhabiting it.

North of the Saco River in Maine, the colonists found densely wooded areas. Vermont, New Hampshire, and Maine had lush growths of beech, yellow birch, and maples. Red spruce and balsam fir grew in the mountains and swamp areas. To the south, in Connecticut, Rhode Island, and eastern Massachusetts, black, red, and white oaks, chestnuts, and hickories abounded. Western Massachusetts and southeastern New Hampshire had a mixture of all these trees. Some areas in the south – especially around Cape Cod – had sandy soil, where pitch pines, bear and post oaks, hollies, bearberries, and prickly pears grew abundantly. All along the New England coast, the colonists soon discovered that the shoreline would provide one of their most important sources of food – cod, sturgeon, salmon, oysters, clams, lobsters, mussels, and other fish and shellfish.

The native peoples, who had inhabited the area for 10,000 years, had adapted to seasons of abundance and seasons of want by devising a mobile way of life. North of the Saco, the Micmacs, Abnakis, Penobscots, Passamaquoddys, and Malecites moved to the shore to begin fishing at the arrival of spring. Women and children collected scallops, clams, mussels, and crabs along the shore. Men used their weirs and nets to catch brook trout, smelt, striped bass, and flounder. Larger catches – such as sturgeon and salmon – were harpooned. Alewives, ducks, and other migratory birds were important food sources, not only for their meat but also for their eggs. In late summer, abundant growths of strawberries, raspberries, and blueberries supplemented the natives' diet of fish and fowl. By fall, the groups relocated their villages to inland creeks where they found good supplies of eels, and during the winter months, the men hunted beaver, caribou, moose, deer, and bear. Over centuries of such life, the native Americans came to accept the hunger they experienced in February and March when game was scarce. The sparse human population – no more than perhaps forty people per square mile – wrought few changes on the landscape.

To the south, however, some changes were evident. The population was much larger at about 285 people per square mile, and here, hunting and gathering coexisted with agriculture. Each spring, villages of Wampanoags, Niantics, Narragansets, Massachusetts, Pequots, and other tribes moved to the fields which the women worked with hoes made of clam shells. In small mounds, they planted five or six grains of corn, alongside kidney beans, squash, pumpkins, and tobacco. This type of multi-crop farming in a single field made weed control more easy. It also kept the soil from exhausting as quickly as it does in single-crop fields. While the women worked their crops, the men fished and hunted. After the harvest, the villagers dispersed into smaller bands and spread throughout the area. The men hunted for days on end, while the women butchered the game and either prepared it for immediate consumption or preserved it by smoking. During the winter months, the hunting bands gathered in forests where they found abundant supplies of wood for their fires.

To increase the amount of tillable land, the Native American women burned underbrush and trees, leaving the dead trees in the fields until they toppled on their own. After eight or ten years of planting, the soil lost its fertility, and the villages were moved to new areas where the women began the clearing process again. Burning the underbrush in the forests was not only useful in clearing land for planting: it also attracted game into the area. The thinned woods were a haven for small game and deer, and were rich sources for wild berries.

While the native American tribes moved from place to place to take advantage of whatever game was available or, in southern New England, to plant

INTRODUCTION

in newly cleared fields, the English colonists stayed where they first settled. This permanency represented a change in land-use patterns, and until the colonies were well established, it created problems for the new residents. Spring and summer were times of abundant resources in New England, and descriptions of the area sent back to England often depicted these seasons. Yet colonists relying on these accounts soon learned to their cost that they needed to bring stores of food to last a year or more, until crops could be harvested. Unlike the native population which moved to wherever food could be found, the colonists remained tied to one location, where they sometimes starved in winter.

To the colonists, the native Americans seemed like the beggars of England, they had so few material possessions. This perception failed to take into account the fact that the tribes owned only what they could easily move from one location to another. The colonists could not understand this mobility or the supposed poverty in which the native Americans lived. Where were their towns, their farms bounded by neat rock walls? The natives were surely a lazy people. With so much abundance around them, how could they fail to show material signs of wealth? The men were particular targets for this criticism. They hunted and fished – which the colonists regarded as leisure-time activities – while the women planted and harvested crops, which the colonists considered the only real work the native Americans did.

The colonists believed that since the natives had not fenced in their land or built permanent towns on it, they had no claim to it. Only the fields which the women worked were seen as private property. In the tribal view, the *sachem* – the village leader – held possession of the territory. While individual families worked specific fields year after year, their ownership extended only to the use of the fields – and to what they could grow in them. To the English, the clam banks, ponds, and hunting grounds that the natives used contained no improvements: therefore they did not belong to the Indians. To the native Americans, the clams, the fish, and the game were their possessions once they

caught them, and they had rights to use the land or waters to catch their game.

In one early sale of land, the Agawam village in central Massachusetts transferred to William Pynchon a tract of land along the Connecticut River. The deed, which thirteen members of the village signed, retained for the native Americans the rights to hunt and gather on the land, and rights to their fields of corn planted there. Pynchon was given the right to setttle there and use the land in a similar manner. But the English interpreted such land transactions as a transfer of ownership, including full rights to sell the land to others.

The nomadic nature of native American life was unfathomable to the English colonists. The fact that the men spent their days hunting and fishing were seen as signs of their inherent laziness. But even more abhorrent to the colonists was the apparent immorality of the natives, as evidenced by their clothing – or lack thereof during the summer – and their "heathen" religion. To "civilize" the native Americans, missionaries established over ninety "praying towns" in New England during the colonial period. Here, they hoped to draw the natives away from their "barbarous" life into a Christian society based on agriculture. Town leaders meted out heavy punishments for infractions of English law such as "powwowing," wearing long hair, polygamy, fornication, or failure to observe the Lord's Day.

The colonists attempting to convert the native Americans to Christianity and to a European lifestyle often annihilated their potential converts. European diseases spread like wildfire through their villages. Twenty or thirty thousand years before the European colonists arrived, ancestors of the New England peoples crossed the Bering Straits into North America. Over the centuries, immunities were not passed from one generation to the next because no exposure to deadly diseases had ocurred. This lack of exposure was due to the small size of the population, the nearly arctic climate in which the people lived for long periods, and the lack of domesticated animals to serve as hosts for disease. Typhus, yellow fever, diphtheria, influenza,

measles, chicken pox, mumps, and smallpox were deadly diseases against which the native peoples had no immunities. In Plymouth, Massachusetts, nearly the entire Patuxet tribe was wiped out by disease between 1616 and 1618. In New Hampshire and Vermont, the Abnaki people died at incredible rates; their population of 10,000 dwindled to about 500 within the first 75 years of English settlement. A 1633 smallpox epidemic spread through southern New England, killing as many as 95 percent of the population. Throughout New England, the total native American population had fallen to about 12,000 by the last quarter of the seventeenth century. To combat disease, the native Americans used traditional cures, such as sitting in sweat lodges, but the treatments had little positive effect and, in some cases, probably exacerbated the disease. The ever dwindling native population – by some estimates 1.5 percent of the New England native Americans died each year from disease – altered the intricate network of families and clans that played such an important role in the tribal way of life. Elders who retained the tribes' history in memory died alongside upcoming tribal leaders. Young women died before they bore children and before they could plant or harvest the annual crops on which the tribes relied so heavily. In the face of such adversity, the native Americans' religious beliefs fell prey to the "civilizing" attempts of European missionaries.

To lesser degrees, alcohol and guns wrought permanent changes on the native culture. To obtain rum, the native Americans trapped or killed game for trade with the English. Armed with guns, they could kill more game, quickly depleting large areas of deer and beaver. By introducing European goods into the native culture, the fur trade eventually broke down many native traditions and standards. When beaver and other animals trapped for their pelts were depleted in New England the traders moved west, leaving behind them native groups that had become heavily dependent on the European trade.

Native American influences on English colonists were prevalent. Into the English language came words such as *maize, squash, musketoes, moccasin,* and *succotash.* In New England, more than 5,000 place names came from the native peoples. Early colonists often lived for a season or two in wigwams, until they could afford the expense and time to build permanent clapboard and shingle houses. To a great extent, the native American's misfortunes aided the colonists who often located their settlements on the sites of native villages that had been wiped out by disease.

Native food was most important to the New England colonists. The local people taught them how to grow corn, beans, and squash, how to harvest sassafras and ginseng, and how to tap maple trees for syrup. Also important were the native methods of catching fish using weirs, spears arrows, and nets.

But for all such transfers of culture, the native Americans of New England were set on a path to destruction with the arrival of the first English fishermen in the north. Before long, they saw seaports spring up where once they spent time fishing. They saw their forests depleted of game through overhunting for trade with the English where once abundant populations of deer and beaver made their homes. In the years between 1600 and 1630, native Americans, especially of southern New England, were reduced to a sedentary life at fortified sites or they moved west. By the end of the seventeenth century, the bountiful landscape they had inhabited for 10,000 years was overrun by farmers and their fences.

TURBULENT BEGINNINGS

The Pilgrims selected John Carver to be the first governor of Plymouth Plantation. Facing page: Carver meeting with the Wampanoag Chief Massasoit. Carver lived only a few months after arriving in America. He was succeeded by William Bradford who served as governor from 1621 and 1656, with a break of only five years.

The first European settlers of New England were a motley crew. Pilgrim separatists, pragmatic Puritans, fishermen and woodsmen, all contributed their unique characteristics to a blend that is the New England spirit.

If the settlers themselves were a varied lot, so too were their experiences in colonizing the New World. In northern New England, explorers, fishermen, and woodsmen established commercial fishing colonies as early as 1607. Most of these settlements were temporary fishing bases rather than full-fledged colonies. Not until 1620 did permanent settlers arrive in New England. Settling in Plymouth, Massachusetts, the Pilgrims formed the first permanent colony in the region. Ten years later, Puritans were leaving England by the thousand, quickly establishing the towns of Cape Ann, Charlestown, Watertown, Boston, Roxbury, and Dorchester in Massachusetts.

Their reasons for settling in the New World distinguish the colonists in northern New England from those in the south. The northern colonists came to fish, to chop wood, and to make money doing so. The Pilgrims came to the New World in order to separate themselves from an English society they saw as evil, heading for the New World when the English king started his campaign to rid the country of Puritan influences.

No matter what their reasons for settling in the New World, the colonists had in common their reliance on England for money, for food, and for defense against claims by native Indians and the French. As a small part of the growing English empire, the colonies were affected by events on the European continent. When England waged war with Spain or France, fighting extended to the colonies, and much of the early violence in New England was due to the European wars.

Beginning in 1605, Samuel de Champlain, a captain in the French navy, sailed along the coast of present-day Maine and New Hampshire. During one expedition, he joined forces with the Algonquin Indians in an attack on the Iroquois. His two tiny settlements, at Quebec and Port Royal, were the earliest in the north.

Right: fugitive Puritans fleeing persecution.

11

CHAPTER ONE

Colonists along the coast of northern New England, in Maine and New Hampshire, created a string of commercial fishing bases that profited from the abundant catches to be netted just off the shoreline. Initially the settlements in northern New England were populated only in times of good fishing, the settlers often returning to England during the winter months. Before long, however, financial backers decided to make the bases permanent, peopled with year-round settlers in order to avoid wasting valuable time in yearly crossings of the Atlantic Ocean.

Captain John Smith, the English explorer who had successfully colonized Jamestown, Virginia, roamed up and down the New England coast mapping it as he traveled. Even before Prince Charles named the area that Smith explored "New England," the English attempted to settle their new dominion. The rugged individuals who established a base at Sagadahoc, Maine, in 1607, were fishermen – not Puritans trying to establish an ideal world or Pilgrims separating themselves from English society. Coming from the seaports of western England – from Cornwall, Dorset, Somerset, and Devon – the fishermen created small villages all along the northern coast at Monhegan Island, Damariscove and Pemaquid, Winter Harbor, the Isles of Shoals, Piscataqua, Spurwick, Brunswick, and Penobscot. But these bases where sailors dried their catches and repaired their boats and nets were not their year-round homes. Usually the settlements were abandoned during the winter months and then revived again at the coming of spring when

catches improved.

Jesuit missionaries from France attempted to settle Maine in 1614 and to convert the area's natives. Establishing a colony called Saint Saveur, these holy men cared little that they were inhabiting English territory. Soon, though, they were expelled from the area by Captain Samuel Argall, who, on behalf of the Jamestown, Virginia, settlers, was fishing in the northern waters.

Two of the men most prominent in the permanent settlement of northern New England were Sir Ferdinando Gorges and Captain John Mason. These two aristocrats sought to establish a type of feudal society in which farmer-fishermen would work the land, fish the abundant waters, and provide England with a good piece of the fish trade. Mason received his first grant from the Council for New England, headed by Gorges, in 1621. The next year, Gorges and Mason obtained a grant for five more tracts of land between the Merrimack and the Kennebec rivers. Forming the Laconia Company,

the proprietors sent two groups of men, one led by Edward and William Hilton and the other by David Thomson, to the New World. The Hiltons established a fishing colony at Dover Point. Thomson built a house in the area that came to be known as Rye, but after only two years he moved to an island in Boston Harbor. Although successful settlements were founded, the financiers of the Laconia Company grew exasperated at the small profits. Mason and Gorges dissolved the company, and in 1629 they divided their holdings along the Piscataqua River.

Mason's only grandson who lived to maturity, Robert Tufton, inherited the American holdings, but it was several years before the new proprietor pressed his claims, and during the lapse of active leadership, the inhabitants of the Piscataqua snatched up land and property. These individuals became New Hampshire's "merchant oligarchy," powerful men who later fought with Massachusetts authorities over control of the area.

In Maine, Gorges created a form of government for the settlements that seemed overly organized for such small towns. Land was divided into "bailiwicks," "hundreds," and "parishes." He established the seat of government at Agamenticus, which he named "Gorgeana" and in which he installed forty-three town officials and a diocese of the Church of England. Gorges never saw his Province of Maine, for which he held such high hopes. He died in 1647, but his vision was inherited by others.

Robert Trelawney established yet another fishing village at Richmond Island in 1631. Trelawney's agent, John Winter, chose a tip of Spurwick (now Cape Elizabeth) as his base and evicted from the area a small contingent of fishermen led by George Cleeve. Cleeve and his men repaired to what is now called Falmouth. By 1638, sixty men inhabited Winter's fishing base. Most, of course, worked in the fishing industry, but a few performed the necessary farming to tide the colony over during months of little fishing activity. The colony prospered until about 1640 when a decrease in

An 1854 woodcut of the abundant waters off New England's coast holding huge numbers of blue fish, which the fishermen are catching. Soon after permanent settlement, northern New Englanders developed a thriving trade with the other American Colonies and southern European countries. With the produce from the American Colonies, England took a large portion of the fish trade away from her competitors.

CHAPTER ONE

A Currier and Ives lithograph of 1876 gives a romantic portrayal of the landing of the Pilgrims at Plymouth Harbor. In the background, the Mayflower rocks gently on peaceful seas.

immigration to the colony's market areas – Massachusetts and Virginia – lessened the demand for its catch.

Captain John Smith was enraptured by what he had seen during his explorations of Maine, and he persuaded the Crown to establish permanent colonies of fishermen there. The quantity of fish exported from the area would increase, he argued, if men spent the entire fishing season at work rather than wasting time crossing the Atlantic. Smith also hoped that the Maine colonies would capture a

large part of the fish trade away from the Dutch, who monopolized the trade in southern Europe. Sadly, like Gorges, Smith never realized his dream. His attempts to colonize Maine were thwarted by bad weather, French privateers, and mutinous crews.

Christopher Levett, a naval captain and member of the Council for New England, also tried to establish settlements in Maine. After depositing ten men at Casco Bay, Levett returned to England in 1624 to garner support for yet another settlement.

14

Right: a Sorony and Major lithograph depicting the landing of the Pilgrims at Plymouth in 1620. Given the length of their journey and the hardships they encountered, the real-life Pilgrims were no doubt a good deal more unkempt and weary upon their arrival.

Overleaf: "Signing the Mayflower Compact, 1620" by J.L.G. Ferris. Binding the Pilgrims in a "Civil Body Politic," the Mayflower Compact was a necessary social covenant that governed the Pilgrims and the numerous "strangers" – people not of the Pilgrim faith – who immigrated to America with them. The Pilgrims had landed at a site far from their original destination, and several passengers argued that they were not bound by the laws of any existing government. The Compact was drawn up to redress this.

The men left behind however, soon abandoned their tiny colony, probably moving into one of the other villages nearby. Levett was never able to raise the money he needed for further settlement. He did return to New England, six years later, but died at sea on his voyage back to England.

While the founders of northern New England placed their hopes for their colonies' success on fishing, this did not remain the area's only enterprise for long. Taking full advantage of the numerous waterfalls and rapids, the settlers soon established lumbering and mast building as primary industries. As early as 1623, the first water-powered sawmill in America was built near York, and in 1624, England received its first shipment of pine masts from New England.

The British moved into the Vermont area much later in the seventeenth century. Captain Jacobus de Warm led a group of explorers who built a trading post at Chimney Point in 1690, but the few settlers did not stay long. The next attempted settlement in the area came in 1724, when Fort Drummer was

erected near the southeast border of Vermont. A decade and a half later, three Massachusetts families moved north of the fort to Charleston.

The investors in the early settlement of northern New England were an ambitious lot. They saw the area as a valuable holding for England. Money could be made in fishing and lumbering, and by permanently laying claim to the area, England could take away from her rivals a large part of the fishing trade. All the financiers needed were men and money, but that was the problem. Finding enough people willing to brave the harsh conditions of Maine, New Hampshire, and Vermont, and enough wealthy investors to finance such risky enterprises, was no easy matter.

The rugged fishermen and woodsmen of Maine, New Hampshire, and Vermont do not conform to our twentieth-century stereotypes of New Englanders. Unlike the settlers of southern New England, they did not come to escape religious persecution or to establish religious communities in a New World. Many of the northern settlers had no intention of staying in America permanently. Instead, they signed on with one or other of the fishing companies for a specific time and for specific wages. They planned to, and often did, return to their homes in England after their terms of employment ended. These colonists were primarily interested in commercial ventures – fishing for fish, not for souls. Before long, though, the Puritan fever was destined to come to this area as well.

In southern New England, religious motives for settling the New World prevailed. In 1620 a small band of Puritan separatists – the "Pilgrims" – landed at Provincetown Harbor and within a few weeks had settled at Plymouth. This migration was not their first. Leaving England, mostly from Scrooby, in 1607, the Pilgrims first settled in Holland, where they enjoyed a society that generally accepted all sorts of religious differences. During their decade in Holland, however, they became dissatisfied with their life. As refugees in a foreign land, they were concerned that their children were losing their English character and Puritan values. Added to this, they suffered economic setbacks on their arrival in

CHAPTER ONE

Holland. In 1620, after striking a bargain with the Virginia Company (or the "Adventurers"), a group of London merchants, the Pilgrims had the capital necessary to leave their temporary home, and one hundred and two adventurous souls set sail in the *Mayflower* for the New World, where they hoped to establish a kingdom of God on earth.

The nine-week voyage to the New World was not harmonious. Among the Pilgrim passengers were many "strangers" – individuals who bought into the voyage, but not into the Pilgrims' religion and way of life. In fact, the separatists made up only 40 percent of the passengers on the *Mayflower*. Reaching America as winter made a harsh appearance, the Pilgrims and the strangers formalized their intent to become a "Civil Body Politic" and agreed to be ruled by laws "most meet and convenient for the general good" by signing the Mayflower Compact.

The separatists and the strangers had different motives for coming to the New World, and the strangers certainly had no part of the religious covenant that bound the separatists together. In addition, the actual site of landing created problems, for the little ship had strayed far north of its original destination in the northern part of the Virginia territory. Plymouth was outside the jurisdiction of the Virginia Company's patent, thus many of the strangers declared that they were bound by no established government. The Mayflower Compact, as a social covenant, was deemed necessary by the separatist leaders to restrain the anarchy that seemed imminent.

The long passage across the ocean and the threats of mutiny upon landing foreshadowed further troubles to come. Nearly half the colonists had died by the first spring, leaving only fifty-two at the time the next ship arrived in the fall of 1621. Food was scarce in the early months, and the Narragansett Indians threatened attacks.

Relations with other Indian groups, however, were good. The Wampanoags, led by Massasoit, signed a peace treaty with the Pilgrims which lasted

CHAPTER ONE

for more than fifty years. Other Indians, Squanto, the last member of the Patuxet tribe that had been killed by disease in 1617, and Samoset, an Algonkin who had learned English from Maine seamen, taught the Pilgrims how to fish, hunt, and farm in their new environment. The settlers interpreted the appearance of these English-speaking Indians as a sign of God's blessing on their efforts, and when they gathered to celebrate the fall harvest in 1621 – a celebration that has come to be called "Thanksgiving" – Massasoit and some ninety Indians attended the feast.

Religion and organization permeated the young colony. "Freemen" – adult male householders – formed the General Court, which was responsible for laws, taxes, and land distribution. "Magistrates" held special positions within the General Court. Chosen annually, these men – the governor and seven assistants – wielded considerable power. Town meetings of freemen were convened regularly to oversee and direct the activities of the

town, and often towns elected "selectmen" to carry out these duties during intervals between town meetings.

William Bradford served as governor of the colony for all but five years between 1621 and 1656. When the colonists first landed, they selected John Carver as their governor, but he lived for only a few months and was succeeded by Bradford. Not only was Bradford a political and religious leader; he was an author and historian as well. His *Of Plimmoth Plantation* recounts the colonists' experiences in Scrooby, Amsterdam, and Leyden, and chronicles the first twenty-seven years of settlement in the New World. In his writings, he was the first to call the group of separatists leaving Leyden "Pilgrims" in comparison to the ancient Israelites and the Apostles.

Bradford and the young colony faced major problems in obtaining a title to the land on which they had settled, and in raising the payments due to the Virginia Company which had financed the

After signing the Mayflower Compact, the Pilgrims debarked from their tiny ship and headed for the shoreline of Plymouth Harbor, a landing reproduced in a pen and ink drawing (previous pages background) and colored engraving (previous pages right). After braving the harsh conditions of the nine-week voyage across the Atlantic and landing at Plymouth Harbor, the Pilgrims faced even greater challenges. In America, they faced months of severe hardship – inadequate food supplies and housing, widespread disease, and constant threats of attack by the Narragansett Indians. Nearly half of the Mayflower's passengers had died by the spring of 1621, when the another group of Pilgrim settlers arrived.

An engraving of Governor William Bradford and Chief Massasoit of the Wampanoags published by Lippincott, Grambo and Company, Philadelphia.

Members of a Puritan family, after an 1876 painting by G.H. Boughton, gaze out from the coast of England toward a New World where they hope to have the freedom to worship as they please. Before 1620, most English Puritans had no thoughts of leaving their homeland, but under King Charles I, worshipping in the Puritan manner became more difficult.

CHAPTER ONE

A Van Dyke painting of King Charles I of England, owned by the Picture Gallery of Dresden. Charles I abhorred the Puritan movement that was sweeping through the Anglican Church. Just as Puritans wanted to purge the Anglican Church of the remaining vestiges of Catholic ceremony, King Charles I wanted to purge England of Puritanism.

Plymouth Rock, carved with the date 1620, is traditionally regarded as the landing site of the Pilgrims in America. This famous rock is one of many historical sites in Plymouth city, including Plymouth Plantation, a replica of the Mayflower, *and the Pilgrims' burial grounds.*

settlement. The first was resolved in 1621, when the Council for New England made a new land grant to the colonists. The second was more troublesome. The colony had grown slowly, sustained by periodic influxes of new colonists, many of whom were "particulars" – so called because they financed their own passage to the New World. The particulars and the separatists clashed over the payments due to the Virginia Company for the colony's growing debts, and over the separatists' desire to bring over more of their group at the colony's expense. When the colony's leaders decided that they must relieve the burden of debt, Issac Allerton and other colonists arranged to buy for £1,800 all the interests held by the Virginia Company. In exchange for control of the fur trade and for greater access to land in the colony, this group – called the "Undertakers" – agreed to pay the Virginia Company £200 a year for nine years.

Still another problem facing the leaders of the small colony was the clamoring by residents for privately held land. From the beginning, the land of the colony was to be held and worked jointly for seven years. Some colonists complained that since they worked harder than some of their fellow settlers, they ought to reap more of the benefits. In response to these complaints, Bradford divided up a portion of the colony's land, giving every man, woman, and child one acre for their own use. The remaining land was still be to held and worked communally, and profits from the communal land were to be divided among the shareholders.

Historian John Demos explored the ever-present nature of religion in his book on the Pilgrims, *A Little Commonwealth*. Religion, he wrote, was simply too basic, too much an assumed constant of life to be rendered fully visible and self-conscious. It registered as a kind of underlying presence, part of the very atmosphere that surrounded and suffused all aspects of experience.

Each Pilgrim town consisted of at least one congregation. The Pilgrims made much to-do over whether members of the town, and congregation, were "converted" or not. Only those who professed

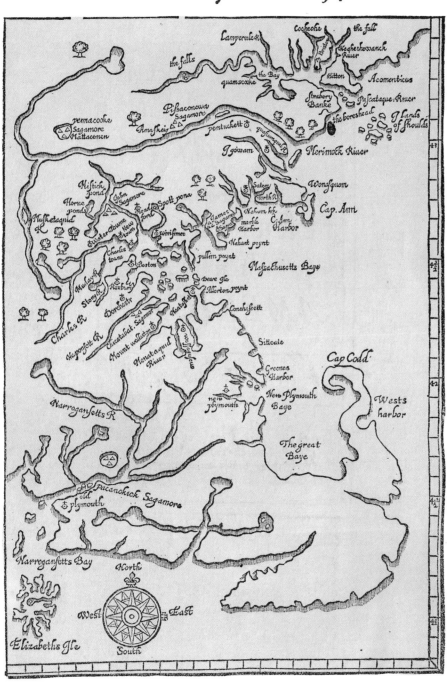

The South part of New-England, as it is Planted this yeare, 1634.

A map of Massachusetts in 1634, printed by Thomas Cotes for John Bellamie. Accounts of the lushness and bounty of New England circulated widely in England and, combined with the attempts by King Charles I to eradicate Puritanism, they encouraged thousands of English Puritans to try their luck in America.

A 1629 portrait of King Charles I by D. Mutens the Elder. King Charles wanted no part of Puritanism, even though the Puritans did not want to disassociate themselves entirely from the Anglican Church. During his reign, he made life so difficult for them that, before long, many began to make plans to move to America.

their conversion or described how God's grace had entered their lives were allowed to join the church. True to the Congregationalist form of Puritanism, each church was independent, and ministers had authority over the worship service and, indeed, over the church members themselves. Excommunication was the punishment that ministers meted out for extremely sinful deeds, while censure was used for lesser offenses.

The original Pilgrims, of whom fewer than 60 survived the first year, were joined by 200 separatists and others during the first few years. The debt taken on by the colony's leaders was paid by 1639, but the colony's start at colonizing a harsh wilderness was shaky at best.

In contrast to the poor and underpopulated Pilgrim colony, the Puritan colony to the north in Massachusetts Bay made a bold beginning in the New World. They came to America in thousands, not in hundreds, and most of the new settlers were fairly well-to-do. As members of England's growing middle class, they had established successful farms and business concerns throughout the country. The Puritans did not want to disassociate themselves from the established Anglican Church in England: they wanted only to purify it, to purge from it the "popish" elements of ceremony. Leaving England – where they enjoyed a large degree of religious freedom and an even larger degree of commercial success – was not a course most of them wanted to follow.

In the 1620s matters changed. England suffered an economic depression. and widespread unemployment Under Charles I, Englishmen enjoyed fewer civil liberties. The king became ever more determined to squash Parliament, and he eventually disbanded it completely, thereby creating an absolute monarchy. In addition, Puritanism was anathema to the king. He wanted to rid his country of the rebellious movement, and as a result, Puritans across England laid plans to leave their homes. In 1629 the Massachusetts Bay Company, founded by 110 Puritan investors, sent five ships to Cape Ann, Massachusetts. The next year, over a thousand Puritans gathered in Plymouth and

CHAPTER ONE

A Puritan couple guard against attacks by Native Americans in a painting by G.H. Boughton.

Early New England colonists, some of them armed, walking to a town meeting in which every adult, white, male church member had a voice in the community's affairs. The Puritan practice of extending suffrage only to church members contrasted with the Pilgrims' more broad acceptance of religious differences among community members.

Southampton, England, and set sail aboard eleven ships bound for the New World.

The Puritan colony was not as tightly bound geographically as the Pilgrim colony to the south. With so many people, land soon became a precious commodity and the Puritan families spread themselves throughout Massachusetts. More and more followers of Puritan beliefs poured into the colony through the 1630s, and the population expanded into new areas.

A notable difference between the Puritan colony of Massachusetts Bay and the Pilgrim colony lay in the matter of enfranchisement. After a brief period of broad political participation in the colony, Governor John Winthrop and his assistants passed through General Court a law declaring that only church members could vote in town matters. This practice contrasts with the Pilgrims' more tolerant attitude toward the numerous "strangers" and "particulars" in their midst. The Puritans soon began to quell any dissension from Puritan orthodoxy, and their increasing rigidity in religious matters led

directly to the founding of a new colony: Rhode Island.

The Reverend Roger Williams was one of the first victims of this rigid orthodoxy. A minister of the church in Salem, he was a strong advocate of the separation of Church and State. He believed that the magistrates should disassociate themselves from religious affairs, and although a given in today's America, the idea was radical indeed to the Puritan mind. The entire Puritan experience in America was aimed at creating "A City on the Hill," a new society led by a government of pious church members. When the General Court tried Williams for his heresy, it found him guilty and banished him from the colony. Williams and a small following made their way to the Narragansett Bay area and founded Providence in 1636. He obtained a charter for his settlement in 1644, and from the time of its establishment the new colony of Rhode Island maintained total religious freedom and the separation of Church and State.

Williams was a remarkable man. Believing in the

essential equality of all men, he was successful in his dealings with the Narragansett Indians. Although he believed that the English had no right to land in America unless they bought it from the Indians (another of the radical beliefs that got him banished from Massachusetts Bay), he did not actually buy land to build Providence: his new friends, the Narragansett Indians, gave him the territory. Until 1675, Williams managed to keep Rhode Islanders and the Indians from fighting. Traveling freely among the Indians, and studying their customs and language, he wrote his famous *Key into the Language of America*, which he published in England in 1643.

A second case of dissension from Puritan orthodoxy in Massachusetts involved Anne Hutchinson and the Reverend John Wheelwright. Hutchinson and Wheelwright believed that each individual received divine inspiration directly from God, without the need for the church's intercession. In their variety of Antinomianism, they believed that God had preordained who would be saved, and that moral conduct on earth had nothing to do with ultimate salvation. In 1637 the General Court tried Wheelwright, found him guilty, and banished him. He and several supporters made their way to New Hampshire. Hutchinson was tried, excommunicated, and banished the following year. She and her followers moved to Aquidneck Island, where Roger Williams helped them secure a grant of land from the Narragansetts. The group settled in an area of Aquidneck Island called Pocassett (which was renamed Portsmouth in 1643). Once there, the new Rhode Islanders again broke into factions and formed new towns. In 1639 a few of the newcomers to Pocassett, William Coddington and John Clarke among them, moved south to form a new plantation at Newport, which thrived and prospered on the active trade passing through its excellent harbor.

Wheelwright's removal to New Hampshire changed the character of northern New England. Long isolated from the Puritan fever, the area had been settled for commercial reasons which persisted until Wheelwright's arrival. The Antinomian minister

A Puritan "church bell." Once in America, where they had immigrated to escape the religious persecution of the English Crown, the Puritans themselves began clamping down harshly on any dissension from their own rigid orthodoxy.

and his followers first stayed in Strawbery Banke (Portsmouth) and then moved to the Squamscot River where they founded Exeter. After buying land for the new town from the Indians, Wheelwright and his followers signed an agreement whereby they proclaimed their loyalty to the king and declared their intention to live peaceably. Only a handful of the families that followed Wheelwright from Massachusetts to New Hampshire were firmly entrenched in Antinomianism. The others were victims of a new law in the Massachusetts Bay Colony that prohibited new immigrants from settling in the colony unless sponsored by two magistrates. America's first immigration law was specifically directed toward this group of Wheelwright's friends and relatives from Lincolnshire whose arrival was anticipated by the Puritan leaders.

Other religious dissenters from the Massachusetts Bay Colony gradually moved to northern New England. Captain John Underhill and his followers

in the Antinomian faith founded Dover. Underhill had been banished from Massachusetts after protesting the colony's treatment of Wheelwright and, more importantly, after engaging in adultery.

As more and more Puritans from Massachusetts settled in the north, they looked to their former colony for protection not only from the Indians but also from claims to the land by Mason's heirs. The settlers of Strawbery Banke and Great Island, New Hampshire, requested annexation to Massachusetts, and by 1641, only Exeter remained independent of the great Puritan colony. The town had grown rapidly since its founding, and Wheelwright's followers were no longer the majority. Since Wheelwright had been banished from Massachusetts, he would have to leave his new home if Exeter became part of the Puritan colony. In 1643, Exeter fell under Massachusetts' control, and all of New Hampshire remained part of Massachusetts until 1679. The enterprising families of Portsmouth began consolidating their holdings, a

Engraver J.S. King depicts an idyllic view of Puritans on their way to worship.

CHAPTER ONE

Left: a call to church in Puritan New England. No deviation from the Puritan ethic was tolerated. Anne Hutchinson, Roger Williams, John Wheelwright and others were banished from the Massachusetts Bay Colony for beliefs that differed from the Puritan norm. They went elsewhere in New England to establish new settlements.

Although never quite as strict with themselves and their children as popularly believed, the Puritan colonists did strive for a godly fellowship of men. Far left: a Puritan father boxes the ears of his son for some infraction of the behavioral code.

large part of which were confiscated from Mason's abandoned wealth. Setting their sights on trade, the Cutts, the Vaughans, and the Waldrons moved quickly into lumbering and ship building, and before long, ships carrying lumber, staves, and fish were making their way not only south to Massachusetts, but also to faraway southern Europe and the West Indies.

Wheelwright and his followers fled to Wells, in Maine, an area divided at the time into four jurisdictions: Gorges's province of Maine, the

province of Lygonia, the Sagadahoc territory, and an area between the Penobscot and St. Croix rivers inhabited by the French. In 1649, after the colonists learned of the death of Gorges and the fall of the monarchy in England, they gathered in an assembly and determined to be ruled under Gorges's original charter, with Edward Godfrey as governor. The arrangement was short-lived. The Massachusetts General Court sent emissaries to Maine to generate support among the colonists for the Bay Colony's claim to the area. Between 1652 and 1658, town

A Puritan governor scolds members of his colony for engaging in Christmas sports.

after town relinquished its loyalty to the Maine government under Godfrey and became incorporated into the York County jurisdiction of Massachusetts. In 1677, Massachusetts cemented its control of Gorges' former feudal domain by buying all rights to his claim from his heirs for £1,250.

Puritan colonists first moved into the Connecticut area in 1635 when several congregations from Watertown, Dorchester, and Cambridge settled in the valley of the Connecticut River. One group, led by the Reverend Thomas Hooker, established Hartford in 1636. In general, the Puritan transplants from Massachusetts were not dissatisfied with the religious orthodoxy of their former home; instead, they sought greater economic opportunities and indeed found them in the river valley's more abundant and lush lands.

Other towns in Connecticut were created when groups of Puritans came from England and settled directly in the area around New Haven in 1638. Within a few years, the New Haven Colony incorporated the towns of Milford, Guilford,

The spectacle of farmers plowing their fields hailed the arrival of spring in New England. The colonists adapted quickly to the new agricultural methods required in the New World.

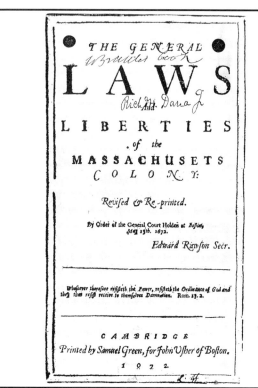

"The General Laws and Liberties of the Massachusetts Colony," printed by Samuel Green for John Usher of Boston in 1672. By the time of this printing, the Massachusetts Bay Colony had expanded to include New Hampshire and much of Maine.

Branford, Stamford, and Southold. Although the New Havenites tried to keep their colony independent, the valley towns were incorporated into the colony of Connecticut when Hooker obtained a royal charter in 1662.

The Reverend Thomas Hooker, a native of Leicestershire, England, had arrived in Boston in September 1633 after spending time preaching in exile in Holland. In the Massachusetts Bay Colony, he served as the minister of the church in Newtown. Along with his congregation, Hooker moved to the Connecticut Valley, and once there, he began expressing his dissatisfaction with the political process espoused by the Puritans. Hooker believed that the Massachusetts government did not provide for enough participation by the populace. He outlined his beliefs in "The Fundamental Orders of 1639," declaring that the government had authority to rule only with the consent of the people, and that consent was given through elections. Connecticut's leaders did not completely heed Hooker's advice in creating a new

A colonial farmer plows his fields behind a team of oxen.

government: instead, they fashioned a government based on the Massachusetts model which limited participation to wealthy freeholders who were members of the Puritan church.

The great immigration abated in the 1640s when the Puritans took over England herself under Cromwell. But groups of families continued to spread throughout the area around the Bay Colony. Determined to maintain Puritan standards, the Massachusetts General Court made a wise decision in the matter of how land would be distributed. Instead of making grants of land to individuals, which was the prevailing method in the southern colonies, the General Court made grants of thirty-six square miles to groups of families. Each family then carved out a plot of land for a house and garden. The court required each town so founded to establish certain institutions that would ensure the continuation of the Puritan way of life. Town governments and churches modeled after the original Puritan form were established everywhere. In these frontier towns, all kinds of craftsmen took

A seal of the Massachusetts Bay Colony in "Nova Anglia."

MASSACHUSETTS
OR
The first Planters of *New-England*,
The *End* and *Manner* of their coming thi-
ther, and Abode there : In several

EPISTLES

Pfal. 84. 3. *Yea, the sparrow hath found an house, and the Swallow a Nest for her self, where she may lay her Young; even thy Altars, O LORD of hosts, my King, and my God.*
John, 4. 21. *Jesus saith unto her, Woman, believe me, the hour cometh when ye shall neither in this mountain, nor yet at Jerusalem, worship the Father.*
Rev. 14. 4. ------ *These are they which follow the Lamb whithersoever He goeth* ------

Tantum intereſt, non *Quaia*, ſed *Qualis* quiſque patiatur. In Tabernaculo *Teſtimonij*, quod erat in Itinere populi Dei, velut Templum *deambulatorium*, &c.
Auguſtin. de Civitate Dei. column. 46. et *Lib* 15. *Cap.* 20. column. 845.

Veſtra autem Pietas, Viri exules, quæ maluit Patriam quam Evangelium deferere; Commodiſque carere temporarijs, quam permiſceri ſacris a Chriſto alienis, Egregiam ſane meretur laudem. Bullinger præfat in comment. Apoc. p. 16.

Boston in *New-England*, Printed by *B. Green*, and *J. Allen*. Sold by *Richard Wilkins*, at his Shop near the Old-Meeting-Houſe. 1696.

275

Tything Men. Captains Commiſſion. 75

Officers that are then to be choſen according to Charter, in Papers as aforeſaid: all which Votes are to be ſorted and numbred with the Proxyes: And the Governour and Deputy Governour being choſen and proclaimed, the eighteen that have moſt Votes, are to be proclaimed Aſſiſtants for the Year enſuing, and other general Officers to be choſen as formerly. Alſo it is Ordered, that every Perſon admitted to be preſent as above, at the opening and numbring of the Votes, ſhall before they enter upon the ſaid work, or be admitted to be preſent thereat, take their Oathes to deal truly in the truſt committed to them as aboveſaid; this Law or Order to ſtand for this year only, as to the manner of Choice.

WHereas you A. B. C. are appointed and betruſted for the opening the Proxies ſent in by the Freemen, and receiving ſorting and numbring the Votes for the choice of Governour, Deputy Governour, Aſſiſtants, and other publick Officers of this Juriſdiction, to be choſen on the Election day; You do now ſwear by the Name of Almighty God that you will deal truly and uprightly therein as alſo that you will not either directly or indirectly diſcover either the perſons or number of Votes until the Election be ended, So help you God. *(margin: Oath to be adminiſtred to thoſe that ſort and number the Votes.)*

The Governour and Company of the Maſſachuſets Bay in New-England.
To A. B. Captain.

WHereas you are appointed Captain of a Foot-Company for the Service of his Majeſty in the Town of B. in the County of E in the Colony of the *Maſſachuſets Bay* Theſe are in his Majeſties Name to Authorize & require you to take into your care & conduct the ſaid Company, & diligently to intend that ſervice by leading and exerciſing your inferior Officers and Souldiers in peace and war, commanding them to obey you as their Captain, and you to obſerve and obey all ſuch Orders and directions as from time to time you ſhall receive from your Major, or other Superior Officer, In Teſtimony whereof, &c. *(margin: Form of Military Officers Commiſſion mutatis mutandis)*

IT is Ordered by this Court that every perſon legally choſen in any Town within this Juriſdiction to ſerve in the Office of a Tything man according to Law, and do refuſe to take his Oath ſhall pay as a Fine to the Town *forty Shillings*, and another to be choſen in his room for that year, and ſo from time to time the ſame courſe is to be obſerved in all Towns. And further, It is Ordered, that the Conſtable of each Town from time to time ſhall Aſſiſt the Tything-men in the Execution of their Office, being thereunto deſired by the ſaid Tything men or any two of them. *(margin: Addition to the Law of Tything-men.)*

Anne Hutchinson faced the Massachusetts authorities when she was brought to trial for practicing an antinomian form of religion. The incident inspired a wood engraving (left) after Edwin Austin Abbey. Hutchinson and her followers believed that each individual received divine inspiration directly from God and that moral conduct on earth had nothing to do with whether an individual was saved or not. For these beliefs, she was expelled from Massachusetts and, in 1638, she moved with a small group of followers to Aquidneck, Rhode Island.

Previous pages bottom right: a page from the law books of Massachusetts, 1679-1680. Shown are sections dealing with the election of the governor and the deputy governor, the formation of military companies, and the "Office of a Tything man." Previous pages top right: the title page from Massachusetts or the first Planters of New-England, The End and Manner of their coming thither, and Abode there: In several Epistles, *printed in Boston in 1696 by B. Green and J. Allen for Richard Witkins. By the time this history had been printed, the Crown had issued a new charter for Massachusetts, incorporating Maine, but not New Hampshire. Plaguing all land negotiations (previous pages left) between the colonists and the Native Americans were differing concepts of land ownership. In many cases, the Native Americans believed they were selling the rights to use land, not selling the land itself, for they had no notion of the private ownership of land. The colonists, of course, interpreted any claims by the Native Americans according to English law.*

up residence, and towns competed with one another in attracting carpenters, tailors, glaziers, masons, weavers, and blacksmiths.

By the late seventeenth century, the younger generation, born in America and with no direct experience of religious persecution, grew less committed to the Puritan church. Although fewer than half the residents of Massachusetts were church members in the 1670s, they, or at least the adult white men among them, were allowed to vote. In 1662, the ever-innovative Puritans had devised the half-way covenant, whereby children of church members were admitted to the church even though they had not professed their own conversions. Since political enfranchisement depended on church membership, the half-way covenant had the effect of broadening political participation. In New Hampshire, after its annexation to Massachusetts, the Puritans relaxed the enfranchisement standards even more. The government declared that all freemen in the New

Hampshire towns could continue their political participation even though they were not church members. Under Massachusetts law, Maine towns were supposed to create town churches and were to adhere to the Puritan orthodoxy. Although the number of trained ministers flocking to the north was large after the founding of Harvard College in 1636, most of the tiny, poor Maine settlements were unable to pay for the services of ministers for several years.

Expansion had its price for the colonists in Massachusetts Bay, Plymouth, New Hampshire, Connecticut, Vermont, and Rhode Island but the price was far higher for the Indian tribes in these areas. In 1637 the Pequot Indians in Connecticut were wiped out. The fighting began when the Pequots killed a few English traders along the Connecticut River. Before long, colonists heard rumors that the Pequots were attempting to enlist the aid of the Narragansetts in ridding Connecticut of the white intruders. A surprise attack by ninety

A group of Quakers being expelled by Massachusetts colonists in 1660. The first Quakers to arrive in Massachusetts were two women. Boston authorities arrested and deported them in 1656.

Connecticut men under the command of Captain
John Mason routed the Indians from Mystic and
wiped out six or seven hundred Pequots – a
massive slaughter of men, women, and children.
The few surviving members of the tribe were forced
into a swamp, where the colonists either killed or
captured them. Those captured were given to
friendly Indian tribes as slaves.

Almost forty years after the Pequot War, King
Philip's War caused the death of about five hundred
militiamen, many civilians, and countless Indians.
The war began in June 1675 when the Wampanoag
Indians, long-time friends of the Pilgrims, attacked
Swansea in Plymouth Colony. The keepers of the
peace for the two peoples – Bradford for the
Pilgrims and Massasoit for the Wampanoags – had
died in 1657 and 1660 respectively. The
Massachusetts Bay Colony joined forces with the
Pilgrims to fight the Wampanoags, who enlisted the
aid of the Narragansetts and the Pocumtucs. After
attempts at negotiations failed, the colonists tried to
capture Metacom, who was the son of Massasoit
and was called "King Philip" by the English. Many
settlers along the frontier fled their homes during
the winter of 1675-1676, and as the war dragged on,
settlers waged war not only with the hostile tribes
but with friendly Christian Indians as well.

In Rhode Island, the colonists hoped to remain
out of the fray, but that proved impossible. Several
Rhode Islanders joined the Puritan troops who
marched across the colony in search of the evasive
Indians. During the Great Swamp Fight, in the
southwestern part of Rhode Island, the
Narragansetts and the Wampanoags who camped
with them were routed. Warfare spread, however,
even into New Hampshire, where the town of
Durham was burned and many families were killed.
Canonchet, chief of the Narragansetts, stormed
Providence in early spring of 1676, and despite
Roger Williams' attempts at negotiations, the Indians
burned the town. Soon, the Indians, never as fully
equipped or supplied as the colonists, were obliged
to return to their homes to take up the necessary
chores – fishing, hunting, and planting – to provide
basic subsistence for their tribes. King Philip himself

Quakers in the New World found little tolerance for their beliefs. New England Puritans barred Quakers from settling among them. Left: John Browne's home, built in 1661 in Flushing, New York, where Quakers gathered despite Governor Peter Stuyvesant's ban on such meetings.

returned home, only to be killed in August 1676. Many of the surviving Indians were sold into slavery and sent to the West Indies, and despite Rhode Island's 1674 law that banned the enslavement of Indians, those who had surrendered to the Rhode Islanders were placed in temporary bondage to the colonists. In Plymouth, Indian children were placed in bondage to the colonists until they reached the age of twenty-four, and adult Indians were banned from the colony. Rhode Island, Plymouth, Connecticut, and Massachusetts Bay colonists faced a long period of rebuilding their homes, but the Indians were permanently dislocated. The Narragansetts, Wampanoags, Sakonnets, and Nianticks moved together to a small area near Charlestown, Rhode Island.

As Rhode Islanders rebuilt their towns and farms after the war, the colony remained a haven for individuals whose religious beliefs forced them out of Europe or out of the Puritan colonies. By 1677, fifteen Jewish families from Spain and Portugal had settled in Newport. Although at first they were

considered aliens and thereby banned from engaging in trade, by 1684 the Jews were afforded full protection of the law.

Other religions had been making their way into Rhode Island from the colony's beginnings. In 1639, the first Baptist church in America began in Providence under the brief leadership of Roger Williams. Soon the church split – forming the Arminian Baptists and the "Five Principle" Baptists. By the 1660s, another Baptist church was created in Newport – that of the Seventh Day Baptists.

The Quaker religion came to Rhode Island in the 1650s. Coexisting easily alongside the Hutchinsons' form of Antinomianism, Quakers soon became the dominant religious group on Aquidneck Island. Elsewhere in Rhode Island, they were subjected to sporadic persecution, but never to the degree they suffered in Massachusetts. The first Quakers in the New World, two women, were arrested in Boston in 1656 and were deported, but eight more arrived immediately. When the Boston authorities banished them as well, Samuel Gorton of Rhode Island

New Haven, Connecticut, was founded in 1638 by a group of Puritans who came there directly from England. Previous pages: an engraving depicting the Puritans' first Sunday at New Haven. Colonists of New haven tried to keep their colony separate from the other larger ones around it, but in 1662 it was incorporated into the new royal charter for Connecticut issued to Thomas Hooker.

In Connecticut, Quaker Humphrey Norton was gagged with a key to prevent him from speaking in 1657. He was sentenced by the court to be whipped and branded with the letter "H" for "heretic" and was fined ten pounds.

invited them to settle in Warwick. Although these Friends did not move to Rhode Island, others came to enjoy religious freedom there over the years. Massachusetts, Plymouth, and Connecticut all enacted strict laws against Quakers, calling for branding, whipping, boring holes in tongues with hot irons, and death by hanging. Rhode Island Quakers persisted in their attempts to spread their message to the other colonies, and many were executed for their efforts. This cruel treatment continued in the colonies even after Charles II banned the hanging of Quakers in 1661.

In Connecticut, the Rogerenes proved more of a threat to Puritan orthodoxy than the Quakers. The Rogerenes were founded by John and James Rogers of New London on the Thames River in southeastern Connecticut. As Seventh Day Baptists, they did not worship on Sundays nor did they believe in infant baptism. The Connecticut General Court passed a series of laws designed to thwart the Rogerenes' efforts to convert new members, but the group had stamina enough to remain active for nearly a century, finally dying out around the time of the American Revolution.

In 1693, New Hampshire passed a law, based on Massachusetts's Ecclesiastical Act, but much more liberal. The New Hampshire act allowed, but did not require, each town to hire a minister. Taxes collected from the townspeople would pay the minister, but those not of the faith established by the town church were exempt from the tax provided they regularly practiced their own religion in a conscientious manner.

Under the control of Massachusetts, Maine was evangelized by a small group of Harvard-trained parsons, among them the Reverend Samuel Moody, who arrived in York, Maine, in 1698 at the age of twenty-two. Preaching to the poor inhabitants, Moody became the spiritual leader of Maine for forty-seven years. He led the church through a period of growth – to a high of 300 members. His fiery sermons and evangelistic techniques foreshadowed the Great Awakening that swept through New England in the 1740s.

Aside from Indian attacks and the increasingly

In Rhode Island Quakers enjoyed more religious freedom than elsewhere in New England. From their settlements in Rhode Island, they attempted to spread their message. Quakers believed that each person could communicate directly with God and that religious ceremony and ministers were not necessary parts of worship. Print by Marcel Lauron.

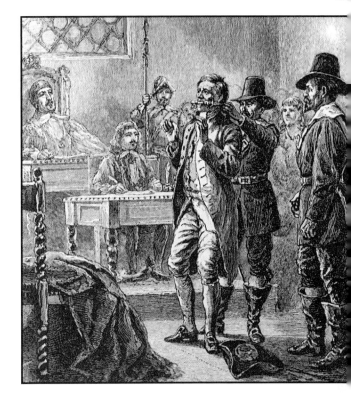

Despite the cruel treatment afforded Quakers, the sect survived. Mary Dyer (facing page) became a martyr of the Quaker religion when she was executed in 1660 on Boston Common. She had been banished from Massachusetts by Puritan leaders, but had returned to continue spreading the Quaker message. In 1945, the Massachusetts General Court appropriated $12,000 for the erection of a statue of Mary Dyer. Right: a woodcut depicting an assembly of Quakers during the eighteenth century.

In all the New England colonies except Rhode Island, unfortunate Quakers were brought to trial in chains (right). Their sentences ranged from branding, whipping (overleaf) and holes being bored in their tongues to death by hanging.

difficult struggle by ministers to keep their followers committed to Puritan ideals, the most serious threat to the colonies came from the mother country herself after the Stuart Restoration. Under King James II, the English Government tried to codify and regularize the governing of the colonies through the establishment of the Dominion of New England in 1685. Designed to centralize the administration of Massachusetts, Rhode Island, New Hampshire, Connecticut, and New York, the Dominion oversaw trade, land distribution, and defense against the French and Indians.

Sir Edmund Andros was named the leader of the council in December 1686. First, he relieved the General Courts of their duties and levied new taxes. Throughout New England, people were alarmed by this act. They saw it as nullifying their rights as Englishmen and contradicting the Magna Carta. When the Reverend John Wise of Ipswich, Massachusetts, led his fellow colonists in a protest against the taxes, Andros jailed him and then made another move endangering the rights of colonists:

he outlawed town meetings except those for the selection of town officials. He also forbade towns from collecting funds to support their ministers, and seized a Congregational meetinghouse in Boston for use in Anglican services. The threat of imposing quitrents further alienated the New Englanders. Andros proposed to tax land titles at the rate of one pound per 800 acres. The tax would apply not only to new titles but would apply retroactively to old ones as well.

Fortunately for New Englanders, James II was overthrown by William of Orange and the Protestants in England during the Glorious Revolution. When the news of the coup arrived, Boston citizens captured Andros and his officials, formed the "Council for the Safety of the People," and reinstalled Simon Bradstreet as governor. These first rebellions by the colonists can be seen as direct links to the much more vocal and prevalent protests of the mid-eighteenth century.

But relations with England never returned to the state of benign neglect enjoyed by the colonists during the 1630s and 1640s. The American colonies were too important to the Crown to be allowed such freedom. England wanted firm control over trade and land distribution. The Crown reviewed charters throughout America, nullifying the old proprietory claims and establishing royal charters for colonies led by royal appointees. In 1691, the Crown granted a new charter to Massachusetts, which incorporated Plymouth colony.

New Hampshire prospered under the new royal charter it received in 1691. At the turn of the century, Portsmouth was a town of about a thousand residents. Forty years later, it boasted nearly 4,500. This growth was due in part to new immigration, but also to the settlement of New Hampshire's interior, beginning in 1713. The new settlements sent farm produce to the residents of Portsmouth, provided flax and lumber to merchants for trade, and became consumers of goods imported through Portsmouth's active harbor. The Portsmouth oligarchy, now rid of claims by Mason's heirs and by the imperialistic Massachusetts Bay Colony, grew more wealthy and powerful. During

CHAPTER ONE

King William's and Queen Anne's wars (from 1689 to 1713), the town was unharmed by the Indian raids that plagued Maine, and its citizens enjoyed economic prosperity that came by privateering and wartime trade.

With the reorganization of the colonies by the Crown, Maine, of course, remained in Massachusetts' jurisdiction. But control of the troubled area was no blessing to the Bay Colony. The tiny settlements in Maine were widely scattered, and because they were not easily defensible, they suffered under constant attack by Indians during King William's and Queen Anne's wars. Life in these frontier outposts was characterized by house burnings, slaughters, garrison life, and poverty.

In 1702, when Queen Anne succeeded King William, the War of Spanish Succession began. Competition between the French and the English over land in America grew ever stronger. After the declaration of war in Europe, Massachusetts' Governor Dudley sought to maintain peace in the colonies. He signed a treaty with the chiefs of the Maine tribes at Casco Bay in 1703, but peace lasted only a few weeks. The English settlements in Maine were destroyed, and farmers abandoned their frontier settlements for the relative safety of the garrisons. In the Champlain Valley, settlers had endured years of hostility with the Indians and the French. For them, there was little to mark the end of King William's War and the beginning of Queen Anne's. When the Maine colonists returned to their farms and villages after 1713, they followed more closely the Puritan standard of close settlement. The Massachusetts General Court, careful to keep dispersed settlement to a minimum, required towns to be resettled by no fewer than twenty families. Despite the difficulty in finding settlers to brave the harsh conditions of Maine, the settlements grew slowly. The lumber industry spread from New Hampshire, where mast supply was dwindling, into Maine. And, since the boundary between New Hampshire and Maine was still unresolved, both

Background: a Quaker family walking to church. In 1659, Quakers settled on Nantucket Island and began farming, fishing and raising sheep. Over the next century their development of the whaling industry there spawned a trade that supplied much of the world with sperm oil.

A man wearing the typically simple attire of the Quaker sect. Members of the sect worked to convert others to their doctrine of "Inner Light," but they were tolerant of the beliefs of others.

Edmund Cheeseman's wife presenting her testimony in an engraving of a witch trial by Darley.

A meeting of Quaker men in 1682.

An engraving, after a work by Howard Pyle, depicting a witch being arrested in Salem. In 1692, an outbreak of witchcraft in Massachusetts, especially in Salem, was crushed by Puritan leaders. By year's end, 141 people had been accused of practicing witchcraft.

Howard Pyle's engraving of a bedeviled girl during a witch trial in Salem.

colonies attempted to solidify their claims to disputed areas by granting townships.

But try as it might, Massachusetts was unable to recreate its colony in Maine. Settlers scattered into separate communities within each township, and town proprietors opened the outlying lands to immediate occupation. The family farm, not the village, became the focus of life in these northern communities. Gradually, as the pioneers cleared more land and produced surpluses, the townspeople established churches and organized town governments. In the New Hampshire interior, where prospering Portsmouth was more easily accessible, towns grew more quickly than in Maine and the Connecticut River valley.

Indian attacks were not the only danger faced by pioneers resettling the interior. Between the Indian wars of the 1720s and the 1740s, diptheria, or "throat distemper," became epidemic, hitting northern New England much harder than southern. Famine, too, plagued the area, especially in 1737. In Boston, it was reported that people and livestock had starved to death in the northern territories.

Relatively untouched by King William's and Queen Anne's wars, southern New England suffered under a different type of war in the 1690s – a war with witches. When Sir William Phips, the new royal governor of Massachusetts Bay, arrived in the colony in 1692, he was confronted with news of widespread witchcraft in the town of Salem. Early in February, the Reverend Samuel Parris's daughter, her cousin, and a few friends had been afflicted with fits. The doctor called in to examine the children proclaimed that they were under the spell of witches. After the afflicted children named their tormentors, local magistrates began hearing testimony against the first suspects on February 29.

The practice of witchcraft and the resulting legal action were not new to New England. Before the beginning of the trial in Salem, some seventy cases had been tried in Massachusetts and Connecticut alone, but only eighteen of the accused were

A painting by T.H. Mattsion, from the collections of the Essex Institute, depicting the trial of George Jacobs for witchcraft in 1692.

By the end of the witchcraft scare in Massachusetts, nineteen people had been executed. Massachusetts Royal Governor Sir William Phips grew increasingly alarmed at the number of cases, particularly when his own wife was accused. In October 1692, he abolished the special court named to hear the cases, and within a few months the epidemic ended as quickly as it had begun. Background: an engraving by F.C. John shows both a male and a female witch on their way to the gallows.

In a woodcut (left) by Douglas Volk, an accuser points her finger at the witch she claims has bedeviled her. In many of the witch trials, no more evidence than a mere accusation was needed to convict a person of witchcraft. In the first nine months of 1692, twenty-six people were convicted.

Before 1692, most people accused of practicing witchcraft were elderly, poor widows. But as the epidemic spread that year, people from all walks of life found themselves being tried in the court of Oyer and Terminer for witchcraft. Lithograph by George H. Walker.

convicted. In Massachusetts the fear of witches did not slowly build into the mass hysteria that existed in 1692. In fact, cases of witchcraft had virtually disappeared in the area during the years immediately preceding 1692. But that year saw an epidemic in full force with 141 people from all walks of life accused of practicing witchcraft.

Before the Salem epidemic in 1692, accused witches were similar in many respects. Nineteen of the thirty-four people accused were extremely poor and elderly widows, and of the nine men accused of witchcraft before 1692, four were without property – either seamen or hired laborers. The first few women brought before the Salem court in 1692 had characteristics similar to those earlier witches, but before long, the community and the court pulled new suspects from among its upstanding, even prominent, individuals. Many of the newly accused were enemies of the Reverend Samuel Parris and his congregation. Some, though, such as Captain John Alden Sr., of Boston, were not embroiled in the tensions between Parris and his

enemies, but had merely criticized the testimony of the afflicted.

Governor Phips established the Court of Oyer and Terminer to hear the ever-growing number of cases. By the time the court first met in June, more than seventy people had been accused of witchcraft. By October, fifty confessions had been made, twenty-six people had been convicted, and nineteen had been executed. Governor Phips, growing more alarmed at the number of cases, abolished the Court of Oyer and Terminer in October, declaring that the Superior Court of Judicature would handle the remaining cases. This court heard accusations against more than fifty people, but indicted only twenty-one and convicted only three. These convictions were overturned the next year, and the remaining cases to be heard were dispensed with by a general pardon. By 1693, the witchcraft epidemic vanished from the legal records, ending as quickly as it had begun.

Disgruntled with the excesses of the witch trials and spurred toward laxity in religious matters by

the new tolerance called for in royal charters, New Englanders became less committed to the Puritan way of life. Despite the efforts of Cotton Mather, the Puritan, preacher, historian, and author of *Magnalia Christi Americana*, by the 1730s most town churches claimed only a minority of the townspeople as members. Arminiansim, which emphasized the doctrine of free will at the expense of the doctrine of predestination, slowly invaded Puritan churches. In Northampton, though, a sudden swing toward religious participation occurred. In a church led by Jonathan Edwards, a young graduate of Yale College, membership began growing by leaps and bounds – some 300 new members in the spring of 1735. Edwards denied that pious behavior guaranteed salvation: instead, he preached that people should actively seek God for a conversion experience. By the 1740s, Edwards' message was sweeping through the land, and a young English minister, George Whitefield, toured America stirring up religious emotions wherever he went. Calling for unity among the various congregations and sects, Whitefield converted his listeners in mass numbers. Nineteen thousand Bostonians came to his revival meeting in the city. In Rhode Island, Whitefield noted that the merchants were too firmly engrossed in commercial affairs to be affected much by his message. He did, however, reach into the communities of Indians and black slaves, and many churches in the region experienced an increase in black and Indian membership. Though he called for unity, Whitefield and the Great Awakening divided the Puritan religions even more. The older generation, and conservatives generally, challenged the emotionalism prevalent in the revival movement, while the younger generation, fired by the flamboyant sermons, coalesced into distinct denominations.

The Great Awakening led to a greater separation of Church and State. Preachers declared that politics tended to corrupt the church. They also saw education as a church responsibilty rather than as a state responsibility, and church-supported colleges, such as Brown and Dartmouth, were established.

CHAPTER ONE

The Awakening also led to a movement that began flourishing in the 1760s: a movement to abolish slavery. Starting among the followers of the Quaker religion so prevalent in Rhode Island, the abolition movement gained momentum throughout the eighteenth century. In these early days, Quakers ceased their participation in the slave trade and in massive numbers freed any slaves they owned.

By 1754, the colonists faced new threats to their survival during the French and Indian War (or King George's War, as it was called in the colonies). From the beginning of settlement in the New World, French settlers and English settlers were isolated from each other, with few minor exceptions. In the 1740s, however, fur traders from Pennsylvania and land speculators from Virginia began to press further west into what is now Ohio, where they came into direct contact with a chain of French trading posts. Although the battles waged during the war had little to do with the boundaries of most New England colonies, as loyal subjects to

the Crown they sent troops to support England's war effort. Massachusetts and New Hampshire sent troops to attack Louisborg at the Gulf of St. Lawrence, and after a fifty-day battle, the French surrendered. Rhode Island, too, was anxious to aid England in its attempts to expel the French. The colony's merchant fleet had suffered attacks by the French for several years, and the resourceful shipping leaders saw an opportunity to increase their wealth through wartime trade and privateering. When peace finally came in 1763, the English received title to all former French holdings in North America except for two islands in the St. Lawrence River. The war left England with enormous debts, and the Crown and Parliament looked to their relatively prosperous colonies for sources of needed revenue.

Before the French and Indian War, the American colonies were relatively free from taxes and trade regulations imposed by the English Parliament, but realizing that the vast resources of America could

Previous pages: an engraving from a drawing by C.S. Reinbart. Dunking was a common form of punishment for those who strayed from the Puritan standards of conduct in colonial times.

During King George's War, a precursor to the French and Indian War, English troops, with the aid of New Englanders, captured the French fort of Louisbourg, Maine, on June 16, 1745. But English possession of the fort was short lived. The treaty of Aix-la-Chapelle in 1748 returned the fort to France. Engraving of the siege by W. Ridgway, 1861.

help England pay her debts, Parliament passed a variety of laws designed to control trade and manufacturing. Not surprisingly, these laws met with loud protests from the colonists.

During the colonial period, most settlers in the north were farmers, but in contrast to the southern colonies where rice, tobacco, and indigo were grown and profitably marketed abroad, the northern colonies concentrated on cereal crops, which had no ready market in Europe. Rye, oats, barley, and other grains were grown in New England, along with pumpkins and potatoes. In winter months, northern families manufactured objects they needed themselves. The small surpluses they created became the basis for shops and trading companies that sprang up even in small, remote villages. In the 1630s Swampscot, Massachusetts, boasted the first tannery in the colony, and shoemakers began settling in Salem and Lynn.

To transport these products and the small

surplus of farm goods, New Englanders needed a merchant fleet. Boston, Salem, Newport, and Portsmouth became ship building centers, which supplied not only traders but fishermen as well with the vessels they needed. Taking advantage of a blessing natural to their area – a great fishing ground between Cape Cod and Newfoundland – New Englanders built the fishing and whaling industries into primary sources of wealth. By 1675, 4,000 individuals were involved in the fishing industry which supplied cod and several other varieties of fish to southern Europe. By the end of the colonial era, New Englanders earned more than $1 million a year from fishing.

Initially, whaling, too, took place along New England's shores. When a whale was spotted, fishermen launched their boats, pursued and harpooned their catch, and then towed the carcass back to shore. As the whale population along the coast dwindled, the whalers began traveling the faraway waters of the Artic and the Azores. In

A street preacher attempts to convert his listeners. After the excesses of the Salem witch trials, the Puritan churches experienced a decline in membership. By 1730, most town churches had only a minority of townspeople as members of their congregations.

exploiting the whales, New Englanders acquired oil for lamps, spermaceti for candles, and other raw goods. In the 1760s, Rhode Island boasted seventeen spermaceti factories, and it became the center for candle trade in the colonies.

A flourishing triangular trade helped the New England colonies prosper. Although the trade took many forms, one variation was trading American products to the sugar growers in the West Indies in exchange for molasses, which was sold to New England distillers for making rum. Rum was then shipped to Africa and traded for slaves, who were taken to the West Indies. In Rhode Island, rum became the colony's major product: at one point Newport alone boasted twenty distilleries. By 1760, 184 trading vessels from the colony engaged in this triangular trade, and smuggling became the means by which the colonists circumvented the duties designed to raise revenue in the colonies.

Through a series of laws called the Navigation Acts, passed between 1650 and the turn of the century, Parliament directed trade from the colonies into England and kept products from other countries from entering colonial ports. One of the laws required that goods from European countries bound for English colonies first be shipped to England before being transported abroad. Other laws were aimed at keeping the colonies in the business of producing raw materials and keeping England in the business of manufacturing products from those raw materials. The Wool Act of 1699, for example, prohibited the colonies from exporting woolen cloth. They could manufacture it for local sale but could not ship the cloth out of the colonies. Soon the colonists were prohibited from exporting hats and iron through the passage of laws like the Wool Act. The Molasses Act of 1733 imposed a duty on molasses imported from the West Indies at sixpence per gallon, later reduced to threepence in the Sugar Act in 1764. That Parliamentary measure was aimed at ending the smuggling of molasses and the accompanying bribery of English officials by trying offenders in vice-admiralty courts.

In 1761, Parliament enacted the Writs of

Assistance, which allowed customs officials to search the homes and warehouses of shipping leaders for smuggled goods even without evidence or court orders. While such searches had been carried out during King George's War without protest, they seemed to violate the civil liberties of the colonists once the war was over.

Fur traders in the north were angered by the Proclamation of 1763, which outlawed any English settlement beyond the Appalachian Mountains and which restricted trade with the Indians to licensed traders.

Even before the Treaty of Paris that ended the French and Indian War, Parliament had attempted to control the exportation of some items from the colonies. The New England Woodlands policy prohibited the cutting of any tree of twenty-four inches in diameter or more that was not on private property. Such trees were reserved for the Crown's use in ship building. The policy was poorly enforced until 1705, when Parliament named

ALL thofe who prefer the Glory of bearing Arms to any fervile mean Employ, and have Spirit to ftand forth in **Defence** of their **King** and **Country**, againft the treacherous Defigns of *France* and *Spain*, in the

Suffex Light Dragoons,

Commanded by

Lt. Col. John Baker Holroyd,

Let them repair to

Where they fhall be handfomely Cloathed, moft compleatly Accoutred, mounted on noble Hunters, and treated with Kindnefs and Generofity.

Previous pages: an engraving entitled "British Resentment or the French fairly Coopt at Louisbourg" allegorically depicts the British victory in 1755. In the picture, the British coat of arms eclipses the French, the British lion keeps his dominion under his paw, and Neptune and Mars join forces to defend the British and Americans. The French force is shown "coopt" in Louisbourg and plummeting down Niagara Falls.

New Englanders responded to the call by the English crown to fight the French and Spanish during the French and Indian War. Above left: a recruitment poster promises handsome clothes, noble steeds, and kind and generous treatment to all men who joined the fight. George Washington's troops constructed a fort at Great Meadows in western Pennsylvania during the French and Indian War. Called Fort Necessity, it was surrendered to the French on July 3, 1754. Left: an engraving by H.B. Hall, 1856.

After the French and Indian War, New Englanders went home to their seasonal chores of sowing, tending and harvesting crops. But relations between the Colonies and England never returned to pre-war status. England had enormous debts to pay, and the Crown looked to the Colonies for needed revenue.

In northern New England, cereal crops predominated, but the colonists there found few markets for their surpluses.

Jonathan Bridger surveyer general. Woodsmen throughout Maine and New Hampshire quickly found that Bridger intended to uphold the policy, and they faced harsh treatment when found in violation of the law.

The ever-increasing attempts by the English to control trade in America led to further conflicts, culminating in 1776 with the colonies' Declaration of Independence. More and more colonists were coming to believe that the burden of taxes imposed on them by Parliament was contrary to their rights as Englishmen. As James Otis wrote in *The Rights of the British Colonies Asserted and Proved,* each colonist ought to be "free from all taxes but what he consents to in person, or by his representative." The conflict over representation stemmed in part from cultural differences that had grown up between the English in Great Britain and those in the colonies. To those living in Great Britain, "virtual" representation held special meaning: each member of Parliament represented the entire English empire. The colonists stood for "direct"

Commander James Abercromby preparing to attack Fort Ticonderoga in July 1758 during the French and Indian War, after a painting by F.C. John. Defeated in the battle, Abercromby was subsequently recalled to England.

A woodcut of Dutch colonists landing on Manhattan Island. South of New England, other colonies prospered. Some were religious communities, such as Lord Baltimore's Catholic colony of Maryland. Others were established for trade and commerce, such as the Dutch settlement on Manhattan Island.

Left: a Quaker couple of the early nineteenth century.

representation and had so from the beginning of settlement in America when members of general assemblies were elected to represent the districts in which they lived. Although various colonial assemblies drew up official protests and groups of merchants organized boycotts, it was not until the passage of the Stamp Act in 1765 that the American colonies were set on their course to independence.

Oats were an important crop in New England and the harvest was substantial. Far left: a five-foot-ten-inches-tall man stands proudly beside his prize bundle of oats.

Colonists continued to rely on trade with England and Europe. In an engraving by M. Haider, two women bargain with a trader for a bolt of cloth.

A colonial settlement on New England's coast.

CHAPTER ONE

A New England colonial village.

Historic Old Sturbridge Village in Sturbridge, Massachusetts, has been preserved as a living museum of Puritan settlement. The 200-acre site includes more than forty restored buildings, including Minor Grant's general store.

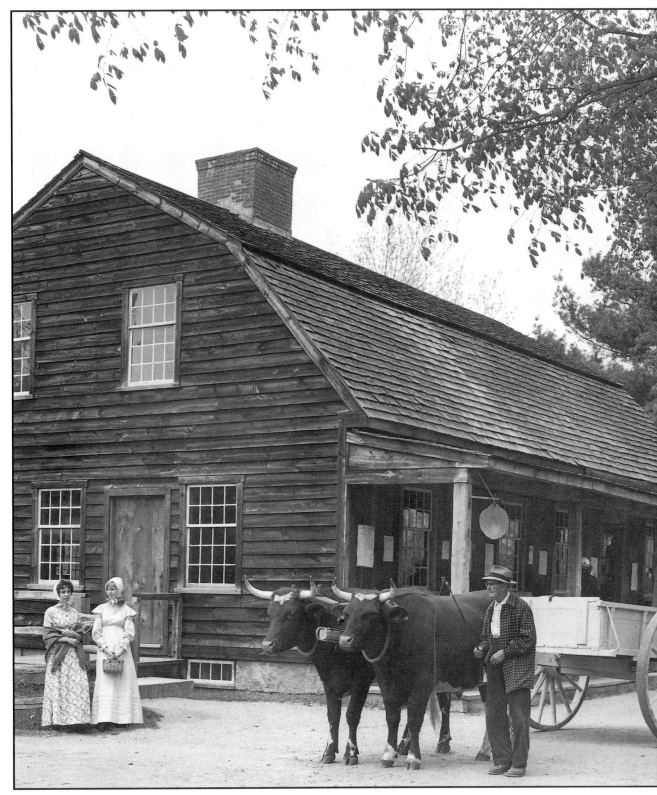

INDEPENDENCE!

Facing page: the British General Lee's cavalry troops at the Battle of Guilford.

The year 1765 saw the diverse colonies join forces in protest against England. Prior to that year, the colonies had acted independently, often competing with one another for land and trade. But the crisis surrounding the Stamp Act created a solidarity among the colonies they had never before mustered. The act placed a tax on colonial newspapers, legal documents, licenses, and other printed materials. Parliament had instituted just such a tax in England and had been successful in raising £100,000 each year. It planned to use the projected £60,000 raised in America for colonial defense.

What occurred in the colonies was an organized protest. The colonists at first ceased any business transactions that would require stamps; then as they grew bolder, they simply carried out their business without bothering to obtain the required stamps. At the urging of Massachusetts, political leaders in the colonies gathered during the summer of 1765 at a Stamp Act Congress where they formalized their protests in resolutions to Parliament. Boston witnessed the first stirrings of violence that summer, when a group called the "Sons of Liberty" incited a riot, looted the houses of the stamp master, and Thomas Hutchinson, the lieutenant governor, and destroyed government records.

Parliament had not foreseen the strong reaction the colonists would have against the Stamp Act. The problem was, first, that the law called for a direct tax. Parliament's earlier attempts to raise revenue in the colonies had been through duties on items of trade. Now, however, Parliament had crossed the line into taxing directly the activities of the colonists. The tax itself was a heavy burden. A liquor license, for example, carried a tax of twenty shillings; a will, five shillings; a newspaper advertisement, two shillings. But above all, the colonists, especially the lawyers, merchants, newspaper editors, and clergymen most affected by the law, were angry because the tax had been imposed without their own consent, or consent by their representatives.

Protesting against their treatment by Parliament and the Crown was not new to the colonies. It had begun back in the seventeenth century, when

The Old South Meeting House (right) in Boston, gathering place of protesters and Patriots in Massachusetts, was the site of the famous meeting that led to the Boston Tea Party.

no force. To Englishmen, "sovereignty" was indivisible, and Parliament, ever since the Glorious Revolution, was the body that held ultimate power. The colonists, however, did not believe that Parliament necessarily had in mind the interests of those it governed. As Bernard Bailyn wrote in *The Ideological Origins of the American Revolution*: "They insisted, at a time when government was felt to be less oppressive than it had been for two hundred years, that is was necessarily – by its very nature – hostile to human liberty and happiness; that, properly, it existed only on the tolerance of the people whose needs it served; and that it could be, and reasonably should be, dismissed – overthrown – if it attempted to exceed its proper jurisdiction."

In the colonies, the debate revolved around Thomas Hutchinson and John and Samuel Adams. Hutchinson became the lieutenant governor of Massachusetts in 1760. A Boston native distantly related to Anne Hutchinson, he entered politics at

Boston's Faneuil Hall was a produce market and assembly hall where Bostonians gathered to hear the rebellious words of Samuel Adams and other famous Patriots during the Revolutionary War. Engraving by John C. McRae.

colonists mobilized to protest the forming of the Dominion of New England and the rule by the hated Andros. But by 1766, protest held new meaning. Those who advocated submission to the English Government came to represent a world of privilege. Those who advocated rebellion signified a new order of political autonomy based on a heritage of independent Puritan freeholders. Misunderstandings of the words attached to the debate over Parliament's control plagued relations between the colonies and the mother country. Not only was there confusion about "direct" versus "virtual" representation, but the players on either side also used the words "constitution" and "sovereignty" to convey very different meanings. Englishmen thought the word "constitution" meant the entire body of laws, customs, and institutions developed over England's long history. Colonists, however, were much more literal in their interpretation. To them, a "constitution" was a written document specifying a government's powers, and a law that was "unconstitutional" had

Because of enormous war debts incurred during the French and Indian War, England needed revenue. To raise money in the Colonies, Parliament passed the Stamp Act, which required colonists to purchase official stamps to affix to all legal documents, newspapers, and other printed material. Throughout America, colonists protested against the hated stamps, throwing them into fires, as depicted in an engraving after a drawing by D. Chodowiecki.

The speaker's rostrum in the Old South Meeting House.

To protest against the Stamp Act, a group of Massachusetts colonists called the "Sons of Liberty" started a riot in Boston in the summer of 1765. Other colonists met in town assemblies to draw up resolutions of protest. The unrest was captured in a woodcut by Darley.

Angry colonists vented their anger over the Stamp Act on the stamp masters appointed by the Crown. A lithograph by Pendleton, after a print published in London in 1774, depicts the treatment stamp masters received. If not tarred and feathered themselves, they were hung in effigy as mobs of protesters vociferously expressed their hatred of the law.

the age of twenty-six when he was elected selectman and representative to the general court. Representing the interests of wealthy Boston merchants, Hutchinson proceeded through a series of political appointments and came to symbolize the old order.

John Adams, son of a yeoman farmer in Braintree, despised the trappings of high social class that Hutchinson drew around him. As a cogent writer on the concerns of the colonists, Adams came to symbolize a new political order. A cousin of John's, Samuel Adams came to hate the Massachusetts General Court, because he saw it as merely an extension of Parliament. Freedom was the only cause that this member of the Adams family thought worthy of his time and attention. In fact, he was plagued with financial difficulties throughout his life. His strong views about the colonies' future attracted a wide following distinct from the usual group of politicians and newspapermen.

In town assemblies throughout the colonies, men met to draw up resolutions of protest. John Adams was chosen by his town of Braintree to draft a statement of the citizens' sentiments. His "Braintree Instructions" centered on the offending sections of the Stamp Act. First, Adams wrote, the law placed a heavy tax on those who could ill-afford to pay it: ultimately, the tax would destroy the economic base of the colony. Second, the act contradicted the rights assured all Englishmen by the Magna Carta, that citizens would not be taxed without their consent or the consent of their representatives. Third, violators of the law were to be tried in vice-admiralty courts, without a jury. As the "Braintree Instructions" circulated among colonists, more and more people saw them as reflections of their own sentiments, and they persuaded their town assemblies to adopt the instructions formally as their own.

In the colony of Connecticut, however, citizens were bitterly divided over how to respond to the Stamp Act. In general, townspeople west of the Connecticut River believed there was nothing to be done about the act. To the east, citizens were

Shortly after the British troops arrived in Boston, violence broke out. On March 5, 1770, troops killed five colonial protesters in what came to be called the "Boston Massacre." The incident outraged an already angry American public. Samuel Adams led a committee that tried to persuade Governor Hutchinson of Massachusetts to ask the English government to withdraw the British troops. A 1770 engraving of the Massacre by Paul Revere.

The Boston Massacre, in which Crispus Attucks, a black sailor and ex-slave, was killed along with four other Americans. Bostonians immediately demanded the removal of British troops, and by week's end they were gone.

A lithograph of the Boston Massacre on March 5, 1770.

After the Massachusetts House of Representatives published a circular letter that detailed the colonists' anger over the Townshend duties, Parliament dissolved the assembly and sent regiments of British troops to Boston in 1678. Right: an engraving by Paul Revere of British troops arriving in Boston Harbor.

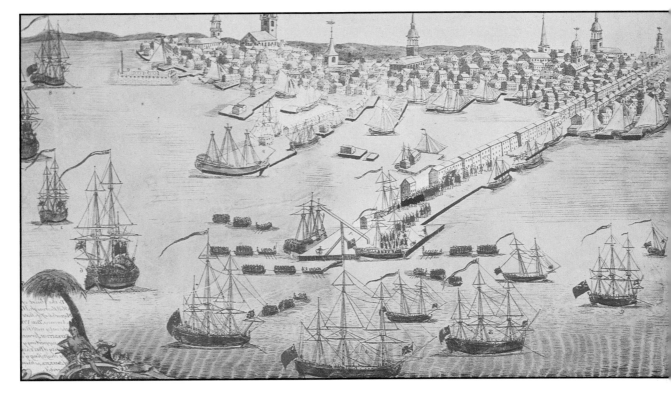

When Parliament passed the Tea Act, granting a trading monopoly to the East India Company to the detriment of colonial traders, colonists again gathered in protest. On December 16, 1773, sixty men dressed as Mohawk Indians dumped 90,000 pounds of tea off the decks of three ships into Boston Harbor. Overleaf: a lithograph of the incident by Currier.

outraged, and in New London, Norwich, Windham, and Lebanon, they gathered to protest the law and to attack Jared Ingersoll, an attorney from New Haven who had been sent by the Connecticut General Assembly to represent its views about the act to Parliament. After Parliament passed the law, he resigned himself to its terms and agreed to serve as the stamp master in Connecticut. Now he paid the price for capitulating to Parliament's desires. During their vocal protests, the townspeople in New London hanged Ingersoll in effigy, and those in Lebanon carried out a mock trial of his effigy and dragged it through the streets.

Rhode Islanders, in their resolves to the Stamp Act Congress, broached new territory in the language of protest. They declared that the colonies were bound only by taxation imposed by their own general courts – not by Parliament. This statement of colonial autonomy was more extreme than the delegates to the Stamp Act Congress were willing to accept, so the concept was not incorporated into their resolution to Parliament.

The colonists were not alone in their protest of the Stamp Act. When they boycotted British goods, even the English in Great Britain began to pressure Parliament for repeal of the act. Almost a thousand colonial merchants had signed agreements of nonimportation, and the boycott hit English pockets hard. In March 1766, under pressure from its citizens in England and its colonists abroad, in March 1766, Parliament repealed the law. The colonists' troubles were far from over, however. On the day the Stamp Act was repealed, Parliament passed the Declaratory Act asserting that, "the colonies and plantations in America have been, are, and of right ought to be, subordinate unto, and dependent upon the imperial crown and parliament of Great Britain; and that the King's majesty, by and with the advice and consent of the lords spiritual and temporal, and commons of Great Britain, in parliament assembled, had, hath, and of right ought to have, full power and authority to make laws and statutes of sufficient force and validity to bind the colonies and the people of America, subjects of the

CHAPTER TWO

crown of Great Britain, in all cases whatsoever" (as quoted in *Colonies to Nation, 1763-1789*).

Realizing the difficulty of enforcing laws calling for direct taxation in America, Parliament resorted to the form of taxation already familiar to most colonists – namely duties on imported goods. In June 1767, Charles Townshend, the chancellor of the exchequer, proposed a series of duties to be paid on lead, paints, paper, and tea. Assured by American Tories that the colonists would not resort to violence, as they had under the Stamp Act, Parliament passed the law. But by then, the colonists were fully prepared to take on this new threat. Boycotts were organized everywhere; in fact, by the end of 1769, the colonies were importing only half the goods they formerly brought in from England. In Rhode Island, many merchants refused to sign nonimportation agreements that first year. With so much of their economy based on trade, Rhode Islanders knew that boycotts would dramatically diminish their wealth. Before long, though, they joined the other colonists in the boycotts.

To enforce the Townshend duties, Parliament established a Board of Customs Commissioners in Boston. Samuel Adams tried to persuade his compatriots to force these officials to resign. Members of the more moderate faction, however, were reluctant to treat British officials as harshly as they had treated the American-born stamp masters. After the commissioners arrived in November 1767, they established vice-admiralty courts, without juries, to try offenders. That the commissioners grew rich, seizing ships and cargoes they judged in violation of the law and receiving one-third of the value of the seized goods angered the colonists even more.

As in their protests against the Stamp Act, the colonies quickly moved beyond boycotts into political rhetoric and action. The Massachusetts House of Representatives sent a "Circular Letter," outlining its reaction to the Townshend duties, to the assemblies of other colonies, requesting responses from them as to how the colonies should respond. Written by Samuel Adams, James Otis,

CHAPTER TWO

Thomas Cushing, and Joseph Hawley, the letter rejected Parliament's right to tax the colonies for the purpose of raising money. The Massachusetts patriots were not prepared for Parliament's next step, which was to dissolve the colonial assembly and to ship two regiments of British troops to Boston. Not thwarted by the dissolution of the assembly, the Boston town meeting called for a convention of towns.

Bostonians bristled at the sight of Redcoats patrolling their streets and camping on the Common. Opposition to their presence mounted until March 5, 1770, when British troops killed five members of an angry crowd in a confrontation that was later called the "Boston Massacre." By the next morning, public opinion had jelled – the troops must be removed. Samuel Adams led a committee which advised Hutchinson to order the troops to withdraw. Finally Hutchinson acquiesced – requesting the commanding officer of the Boston troops to abandon the city. By week's end, the troops were gone, and Bostonians had yet another taste of successful revolt.

Another crisis was soon at hand. In 1772, Parliament proposed to take over the payment of salaries to the royal governors and judges. On the surface, this move should have pleased the colonists, who to that point had been striving to free themselves of the burden of taxes. But the political atmosphere had changed. Now colonists saw the measure as an attempt to control them even more. They believed that the governor and judges would look first to the interests of the Crown, which paid their salaries, rather than to the interests of those whom they were hired to serve. In Boston, by refusing to convene the legislature, Governor Hutchinson did not provide a forum for the debate over salaries. Bostonians, though, had become practiced at circumventing that inconvenience. They created a "Committee of Correspondence" to circulate their views to other town meetings and to request opinions in return. To each town, they sent the "Boston Pamphlet," in which were stated their rights as subjects of the Crown. To Governor Hutchinson, response to the

78

pamphlet provided a rude awakening. He had wrongly assumed that the trouble brewing in Boston was the result of emotions fired by Samuel and John Adams and other "hot-heads." Now he confronted the fact that the population in general supported the Adams' views. What followed was a show-down in the general court early in 1773, in which for the first time the issue of independence versus submission to Parliment was debated in public.

While the Bostonians were generally confining themselves to debate, public disorder and violence had broken out elsewhere. In Connecticut, where the line between those who supported Parliament's authority and those who advocated political autonomy had been drawn down the Connecticut River, colonists waged a political battle that resulted in the ousting of the current leadership. Eastern Connecticut, a stronghold of Puritan values, had few dealings with London. Basically rural and underdeveloped, the area spawned "patriots" such as Eliphalet Dyer, Jonathan Trumbull, Roger Sherman, and Silas Deane. To the west, the colonists carried out substantial trade with England, and the Anglican Church was growing more dominant. The eastern patriots, founding the Connecticut chapter of the Sons of Liberty, were determined to rid the colony's government of those who were so easily swayed to Parliament's authority. Five hundred Sons of Liberty intercepted Jared Ingersoll on his way to Hartford for a general assembly session on the Stamp Act. The patriots forced Ingersoll to read a prepared letter of resignation, not only where they captured him in Wethersfield, but also later in Hartford. With the hated stamp master thus removed from power, the Sons of Liberty then mounted a successful campaign to oust Governor Thomas Fitch, installing William Pitkin as governor and Jonathan Trumbull as deputy governor in the election of 1766.

Following a series of minor confrontations and attacks on property, Rhode Islanders found themselves in the midst of a conflict centered on the inspection of ships. On June 9, 1772, Captain William Dudingston of His Majesty's Ship *Gaspee*

chased the *Hannah* up the Narragansett Bay because he suspected that the *Hannah* was carrying smuggled goods. Having sailed too close to the shore, the *Gaspee* ran aground on Namquit Point near Providence. Leading citizens of Providence, among them the merchant John Brown and Captain Abraham Whipple, mounted a surprise attack on the *Gaspee*. After wounding Dudingston and taking the crew ashore, the Providence band set fire to the ship. Rhode Island's patriots called on Samuel Adams for advice on handling the affair. Because of the newly strengthened laws against damaging Crown property, the raiders of the *Gaspee* would have faced execution if found guilty by a royal commission investigating the event. No one was convicted, but the Rhode Island Tories asked Parliament to send warships to the colony.

Boston did not remain nonviolent for long. In response to Parliament's passage of the Tea Act, Bostonians called a public meeting. The law required that all tea should be sold by the East India Company directly to the colonies through agents or consignees. Duties were to be paid on the tea's arrival in America. Previously the East India Company had sold tea to wholesalers in England, who then sold it to American wholesalers for distribution to local merchants. The new arrangement would give the East India Company an even stronger monopoly on the tea trade, would allow it to reduce its inventory efficiently, and would bring revenues to the Crown through the threepenny Townshend duty on tea. Colonists engaged in the tea trade would suffer, however, due to the prohibition of trade with any tea company other than the East India and due to the limiting of trade to official consignees.

The colonists view was that Parliament should not have the power to grant a monopoly to a private company, and they feared that before long Parliament would tamper in colonial business in just that manner. At the public meeting called by Boston's North End Caucus, consignees were urged to relinquish their commissions. The merchants, including two of Hutchinson's sons, held out. Surrounding towns entered the debate at the

In April 1775, General Thomas Gage, who had succeeded Hutchinson as Governor of Massachusetts, decided to capture the stores of colonial military supplies in Concord. Gage sent 700 troops through Lexington to Concord. In Lexington, the English troops encountered the colonial Minute Men. Shots were fired against the orders of commanders of both sides, and eight Minute Men lay dead. Previous pages: an engraving of the incident after a painting by Alonzo Chappel.

Farmers from all around Concord and Lexington heeded the call to action. Dressed in whatever they had and armed with their own rifles, the Minute Men (facing page) set out to do the impossible: defeat the huge, well-trained and well-equipped British army.

CHAPTER TWO

Minute Men march off to confront the Redcoats in a Currier and Ives print of 1876.

An engraving of 1776 shows Americans boycotting tea merchants and harassing the agents of the East India Company to make them resign their consignments.

The Revolutionary War flags, uniforms, currency and arms of the new American nation.

CHAPTER TWO

After the skirmish in
Lexington, the Redcoats
crossed North Bridge into
Concord, where their target
was the military stores of the
Continental Army.

At the Battle of Lexington on April 19, 1775, eight Minute Men were killed before the British troops continued their march toward Concord.

instigation of the Boston Committee of Correspondence, and a meeting of the people gathered to forbid the drinking of tea. But Governor Hutchinson would not back down. Holding the consignees to their commissions, he refused to allow the tea ships that had entered Boston's harbor to leave until the required duties had been paid.

On the night of December 16, 1773, as many as sixty men dressed as Mohawk Indians boarded three ships and dumped 90,000 pounds of tea into the harbor.

Response to this flagrant act of destruction was quick. By spring, Parliament enacted three Coercive Acts: the Port Act, the Administration of Justice Act, and the Massachusetts Government Act. The first prohibited trade in and out of Boston until the citizens raised money to pay for the tea. The second moved the adjudication of trials of royal officials out of Massachusetts whenever the governor believed that an impartial jury could not be convened in the colony. The third made sweeping changes to the colony's charter, consolidating more power in the

office of the governor while lessening the power held by the general assembly. These laws, together with a strengthened Quartering Act, which allowed governors to confiscate uninhabited, privately owned buildings for housing British troops, were called the "Intolerable Acts" by the angry colonists.

Although the new acts were aimed specifically at Massachusetts, other colonies came to its defense. When the port of Boston was blockaded, beginning in June 1774, the general assemblies of many other colonies – New Hampshire, Rhode Island, and Connecticut among them – voted to send relief to the poor of Boston and Charlestown.

In New Hampshire, Governor John Wentworth, a devoted Loyalist who firmly believed in Parliament's right to pass laws affecting the colonies, tried in vain to keep the citizens of his colony out of the rebellion. John was the nephew of Benning Wentworth, who served as governor from 1741 to 1766. Although he at first opposed the Stamp Act during a three-year stay in England, he soon relinquished such rebellious attitudes – an

action for which he was awarded the royal
governorship in 1766. During his early years as
governor he was popular, but as he attempted to
carry out his official duties, he alienated New
Hampshirites. Woodsmen were dismayed that he so
efficiently administered the Crown's policy of
reserving pines for the Royal Navy. Other colonists
cried out against his revocation of land grants in the
Connecticut River valley.

Wentworth had effectively blocked the signing
of nonimportation agreements until settlers of the
New Hampshire interior had felt pressure from
Connecticut and Massachusetts to join their protest.
By the time of the Intolerable Acts, however, he no
longer had control of the legislature. When he
attempted to adjourn it, the legislature simply
relocated to Exeter. More trouble for Wentworth
was brewing. At the request of Governor
Hutchinson in Massachusetts, Wentworth sent a
crew of carpenters to Boston to build barracks for
British troops. He had tried to hide the fact that the
crew he was gathering would be hired for such
offensive work, but word soon leaked out, and
New Hampshirites were incensed. In August 1775,
Wentworth and his family left Portsmouth forever.
(He did return to North America, in 1792, but in a
new capacity – as acting governor of Nova Scotia.)

The removal of Wentworth was not enough to
pacify New Hampshe. On December 13, 1775, Paul
Revere, during one of the rides that secured his
place in American Revolutionary legend, announced
the imminent arrival of the British ship *Scarborough*
at Fort William and Mary in Portsmouth. Earlier that
year, the *Scarborough* had captured two colonial
ships that were bringing food and supplies to
Portsmouth. Instead of allowing the ships to dock,
the British diverted them and their cargoes to
Boston where the British fleet was stationed. With
the hated *Scarborough* nearing land, 400 patriots
raided the fort where they captured 100 barrels of
gun powder.

After a call for a meeting of delegates from all
the colonies, the First Continental Congress met in
September 1774 at Philadelphia. Delegates soon
reached the conclusion that Parliament had no right

whatsoever to legislate to the colonies. Now it was not only taxation without representation that ired the colonists: it was any British law at all.

Meanwhile, General Thomas Gage, who had taken over the governorship of Massachusetts from Thomas Hutchinson, continued to request troops from England. Already 4,000 regulars were present in the colony, but Gage knew that if a war broke out this number would be inadequate. In April 1775, when he learned that no more troops would be sent, he decided that he must seize the military supplies of the provincial congress stored in Concord. But sending 700 troops secretly through an area already prepared for trouble proved impossible. Paul Revere, William Dawes, and others had already devised a plan by which they could warn the colonists in nearby Charlestown about any movement by the British troops. From his base in Boston, Revere would watch the British troops to determine their route to Lexington and Concord. By raising one lantern in the steeple of Christ's Church,

he would signify that the troops were taking the route over land. Two lanterns in the steeple would mean that the troops were rowing across the Charles River. When Revere determined the route, he asked Robert Newman, who lived across the street from Christ's Church, to raise two lanterns in the steeple. Revere then rode through Charlestown and Mistick, where he awakened Captain John Parker of the Minute Men, America's rough-and-tumble troops.

By morning, the British troops reached Lexington where they found a group of seventy Minute Men occupying the common. Veterans of the French and Indian War, most of these Minute Men were far older than the young, well-trained British soldiers they were about to face. Although both sides were under orders to hold their fire, someone fired a shot, and the resulting chaos left eight Minute Men dead. The Redcoats continued their march to Concord where they destroyed the small arsenal of military supplies left there by the

Previous pages: the Continental army crossing Concord Bridge, depicted in an engraving after a painting by Alonzo Chappel.

British Lieutenant-Colonel Smith and Major Pitcairn used Wright Tavern (left) as their command post for the early battles of the Revolutionary War. The tavern was built in 1747.

The birthplace of John Adams, second President of the United States, in Quincy, Massachusetts. Adams entered the political scene around the time of the Stamp Act. The town of Braintree selected him to draft its protest to the act, and Adams' "Braintree Instructions" cogently summarized the offensive nature of this law. Soon, several other towns adopted his statement as their own.

Paul Revere, silversmith, political cartoonist and famed Revolutionary War leader, drew a cartoon in 1768 depicting the seventeen members of the Massachusetts General Court who at first wanted to quell the protests by the colonists. However, by 1768, the colonists had new cause for protest in the Townshend Act, which placed duties on imported paint, lead, paper and tea.

CHAPTER TWO

patriots. However, as the soldiers returned to Boston, the woods came alive with aggression. Snipers along their route fired from the safety of trees and fences, and before long Gage was forced to send another 1,500 men to aid the returning troops. At the end of the first day of the Revolutionary War, 273 British troops and about 100 Minute Men were dead.

On May 10, delegates to the Second Continental Congress convened in Philadelphia. Without legal authority, but with the knowledge that action was needed, the congress formed the Continental Army under George Washington as commander-in-chief and named John Hancock president.

Born in Braintree, Massachusetts, Hancock had not grown up in the relative poverty of his school friend John Adams. After the death of his father, Hancock lived with a wealthy uncle in Lexington and later attended and graduated from Harvard. Drawn by Samuel Adams into the political activity brewing in Boston, Hancock abandoned the prospering business he had inherited from his uncle in order to devote all his energies to the conflict with England.

Boston was soon invaded by more than a thousand Redcoats along with Generals Howe, Clinton, and Burgoyne. The British generals were quick to make their next move – an attack on the colonial emplacement at Breed's Hill on June 17. With 2,200 troops, the Redcoats stormed the redoubt in a battle called Bunker Hill, but within a few hours, a thousand lay wounded or dying on the field. The Minute Men, after exhausting their supply of powder, were forced from the area where they lost 400 men. Although technically a British victory, King George III was angry that so many of his troops had died in the battle. He recalled General Gage and replaced him with General Howe.

The Continental Congress, by sending the Olive Branch Petition to the king, made a final attempt at negotiation, but before long even the most moderate delegates realized there was no turning back. The congress drafted the "Declaration of the

This French broadside (background) depicted for Europeans the first battle of the Revolutionary War: the Battle of Lexington. The French were petitioned by the Americans for aid to their war effort

On the night of June 16, 1775, the Continental Army fortified Breed's Hill in Boston, depicted in an engraving after a work by Darley. The next morning, the Battle of Bunker Hill was in full swing. The British sent 2,200 troops into battle, and within a few hours a thousand lay wounded or dying on the field.

CHAPTER TWO

Causes and Necessity of Taking Up Arms," in which the delegates declared the need to choose between submission and resistance by force. With great dispatch, the congress commissioned groups of delegates to seek aid and munitions from foreign countries, and established a navy under the command of Commodore Esek Hopkins of Rhode Island. Two ships were outfitted, the *Washington* and the *Katy* (later named the *Providence*), under the command of Captain Abraham Whipple.

To the north, the Battle of Machias brought Mainers into the war. In the spring of 1776, a Loyalist naval captain named Ichabod Jones sailed two sloops to Boston where he planned to trade goods from Machias for much-needed food and provisions. In Boston, he obtained permission from the royal commander to unload his stores on the condition that he would return to Boston with timber and firewood. Sailing back to Machias accompanied by the *Margaretta*, Jones reached his home port in June. There he faced the problem of

persuading the townspeople to accept the bargain he had struck in Boston. Most of the citizens, desperate for food, agreed, but Jones made a grievous error in distributing the provisions: according to some accounts, he sold food only to those who had voted in the town meeting to accept his deal. Angry, and no doubt hungry, the townspeople seized one of Jones' sloops, the *Unity*, and set off to capture the *Margaretta*, After a battle in which five townspeople and the captain of the *Margaretta* were killed, the infant Maine navy moved guns from the royal schooner to the *Unity* and renamed their victorious ship the *Machias Liberty*.

A few months later, Mainers suffered an extremely harsh attack by the British. Ordered by Vice-Admiral Graves to destroy nine harbors and towns northeast of Boston, Lieutenant Henry Mowat sailed the *Canceaux* and a flotilla of six ships into Falmouth's harbor on October 17, 1775. The bombardment began the next day and lasted eight hours. In addition, British troops came ashore and set some shorefront buildings on fire. At the end of the battle, three-fourths of the town had been burned and nearly 160 families were left homeless.

Through the Maine woods, 1,100 American soldiers under the command of Colonel Benedict Arnold marched on Quebec. Their goal was to drive the British from Quebec and recruit the French and Indians living there into the American rebellion. The march lasted six weeks, but when the troops finally arrived across the St. Lawrence River from Quebec, they were joined by troops under General Richard Montgomery. The British drove the Americans back, but Arnold persisted in his efforts, keeping the town under fire for several months. But the American troops soon realized the futility of their mission and withdrew from Canada.

Bostonians continued to suffer the presence of the hated Redcoats. Since the attack on Breed's Hill, the British troops had been contained within the city, but soon the patriot troops began to fortify themselves on Dorcester Heights just outside, and from this vantage point George Washington threatened to fire on the British in Boston. General

4   JOHN ADAMS PROPOSING WASHINGTON FOR COMMANDER-IN-CHIEF OF THE AMERICAN ARMY

Immediately after the battles of Lexington and Concord, the Second Continental Congress convened in Philadelphia. In a 1913 painting by J.W. Dunsmore (previous pages right), John Adams is shown nominating George Washington for the position of commander-in-chief of the Continental Army. John Hancock of Massachusetts was elected president of the Second Continental Congress on May 10, 1775, about a month after the battles of Lexington and Concord. Previous pages left: an engraving of John Hancock from American Magazine. He was the first member of the Continental Congress to sign the Declaration of Independence. Background: a lithograph by Currier and Ives, entitled "John Hancock's Defiance, July 4, 1776," shows Hancock's elaborately fashioned signature.

Left: the Battle of Lexington.

Settlers in Vermont's Green Mountains were plagued by the dispute between New York and New Hampshire over land claims. Under the command of Ethan Allen, the "Green Mountain Boys," a force of some 200 men, were determined to protect the titles granted to settlers by the New Hampshire Government.

Howe did not want to engage the colonists in another fight that might result in casualties as high as those in the Battle of Bunker Hill, and in March 1776 he wisely decided to remove his troops to Halifax in Nova Scotia. Boston was now free from the Redcoat presence, George Washington's troops took control of the city, and for the remainder of the war, little military activity occurred in the colony.

In Connecticut, where the Tory government of Governor Thomas Fitch had been ousted from power in 1766, the new general assembly and Governor Jonathan Trumbull were determined to rid the colony of any Tory sympathizers. The assembly passed laws that called for the loss of property, imprisonment, or death for those with Tory leanings.

Despite the fighting and the protests that were occurring everywhere, Americans had yet to declare themselves free from British rule. Throughout the winter of 1776, an anonymously published pamphlet entitled *Common Sense* had been

circulating through the colonies. When John Adams wrote a refutation of the pamphlet's arguments, the author, Thomas Paine, a magazine editor recently arrived in the colonies from England, presented himself at the Adams' temporary home in Philadelphia. At the urging of Benjamin Franklin, Paine undertook a history of the conflict between the colonies and England. In *Common Sense*, he advised the Continental Congress to unite the colonies under a new charter and to declare independence.

The first stirrings of independence occurred in Rhode Island where the general assembly met on May 4, 1776, to declare itself free of allegiance to the king. (Since 1884, the day has been observed in the state as Rhode Island Independence Day.) In Philadelphia at the Continental Congress, Richard Henry Lee proposed a resolution that the delegates had been tip-toeing around for months:

RESOLVED: That these United Colonies are, and of right ought to be, free and independent States, that they are absolved from all allegiance to the British Crown, and that all political connection between them and the State of Great Britain is, and ought to be, totally dissolved.

The congress then asked Thomas Jefferson and others to prepare a draft outlining the justifications of independence, and on July 4, 1776, the delegates adopted the Declaration of Independence, a document that would change world history.

The celebrations of independence were short-lived in Rhode Island where the British occupied Newport in December 1776. For three years, Newport suffered under British occupation: shipping ceased and half the population of Aquidneck Island abandoned their homes for relative safety on the mainland. In Providence, where refugees poured into the city, food was scarce until Connecticut came to its aid sending supplies that kept starvation at bay.

The Continental Navy under Esek Hopkins was trapped in Providence. After engaging the British ship *Glasgow* in battle, Commodore Abraham Whipple sailed his three badly damaged ships into Providence, and there they remained when the British fleet took control of Narragansett Bay in December 1776.

The first British attack on Connecticut was mounted by Major General William Tryon, the royal governor of New York, in April 1777. Tryon and some 2,000 troops attacked Danbury where they destroyed the Continental Army's supplies. Although a unit of 200 militiamen headed by David Wooster and Benedict Arnold fought to keep the British at bay, the Redcoats destroyed 1,700 bushels of corn and 1,600 tents, an action that would gravely imperil the Continental Army over the coming months as it wintered in Valley Forge.

Connecticut's Governor Trumbull came to Washington's aid during the winter of 1777-1778 at Valley Forge. There, about 3,000 American troops were hungry, inadequately clothed, and suffering under a typhus epidemic. When Trumbull learned

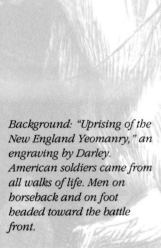

Background: "Uprising of the New England Yeomanry," an engraving by Darley. American soldiers came from all walks of life. Men on horseback and on foot headed toward the battle front.

From the rooftops in Boston, colonists had a view across the Charles River of the action in the Battle of Bunker Hill. Today a monument stands to commemorate the battle in Charlestown. Lithograph after a work by Howard Pyle.

CHAPTER TWO

of this state of affairs he commissioned Colonel Henry Champion to roam through the countryside to gather cattle for the troops. Champion drove several herds to Valley Forge throughout the winter and spring, and it was his efforts and those of Governor Trumbull that made the survival of the troops in Valley Forge possible.

In the spring of 1778, George Washington was able to turn his attention to the occupied town of Newport. Under Washington's orders, General John Sullivan of Massachusetts gathered 8,000 soldiers to attack the British in the harbor town. To his aid came a French fleet under Comte Jean Baptiste d'Estaing, who planned to attack the British fleet from the southwest. D'Estaing managed to expel the British fleet from Newport harbor, but soon another fleet of twenty British ships appeared off nearby Point Judith. When a huge storm caused great damage to the ships on both sides, they withdrew – the French fleet to Boston and the British to New York City. On land, Sullivan pressed onward, reaching Newport in August. But he was not prepared to push the British out of Newport completely: instead, he withdrew and the British counterattacked at Portsmouth. Newport remained under British control until October 1779 when the troops moved south to aid the war effort there.

Maine continued to be a site of confrontations between the Americans and the British. In June 1779, a British fleet occupied Castine in the Penobscot Bay. The Massachusetts General Court sent a thousand militiamen in twenty-four transport ships to the area. The frigate *Warren* led the convoy and the nineteen armed ships of the Massachusetts state navy. During the ensuing battle, the British defense remained secure, and in August the Americans were forced to withdraw. Brigadier General Peleg Wadsworth, the grandfather of Henry Wadsworth Longfellow, emerged from the battle a hero. After the Americans' failed attempt to capture the fort, Wadsworth was named commander of the military in Maine. At his headquarters in Thomaston, he was captured by the British in February 1781 and was taken to the fort at Castine. There, he and a fellow prisoner escaped by cutting through the pine ceiling of their room.

During his winter at Morristown, New Jersey, from 1779-1780, George Washington again called on Governor Trumbull of Connecticut for aid. Although the Commissary Department had undergone radical changes after the near starvation of the troops at Valley Forge, it had become mired in bureaucratic red tape by 1779. Trumbull responded to Washington's request, managing to gather and supply the needed provisions at once.

Before 1781, Connecticut had been under attack by the British three times – at Danbury where the Continental Army supplies were stored, at the Greenwich saltworks, and at New Haven, Fairfield, and Norwalk, where 3,000 British troops destroyed massive amounts of property. Connecticut again saw heavy fighting, this time with much loss of life, in September 1781. The new British brigadier general, Benedict Arnold, with 2,000 men under his command, attacked New London and Groton. Born in Connecticut, Arnold became involved in America's war effort when he was named captain of a New Haven militia company. Along with Ethan Allen, he had captured Fort Ticonderoga and then led the American attack on Quebec. But the British offer of £6,000 and a commission as brigadier general persuaded Arnold to change allegiance and hand over the American fort at West Point. Fortunately for the Americans, Arnold's treachery was discovered before the fort was transferred.

Under attack by Arnold's troops, the fort at New London fell quickly, but at Fort Griswold in Groton, Colonel William Ledyard and 150 American troops held out until the British charged with bayonets. When Colonel Ledyard surrendered, one of the enemy officers killed him with a sword. A massive slaughter resulted, with the British soldiers killing more than eighty Americans. Meanwhile, Arnold's troops across the river at New London set fire to the town, destroying homes, stores, barns, and public buildings.

After the battles in New London and Groton, most of the fighting in the Revolutionary War shifted south – to New York, Pennsylvania, New Jersey, Virginia, and the Carolinas. On October 17, 1781, Cornwallis, pent up in Yorktown, surrendered to the American forces.

"His Britannic Majesty acknowledges the said United States ... to be free, sovereign and independent States." So began Article I of the Treaty of Paris, which formalized the independence of the American colonies from England. The treaty specified the boundaries of the new nation at the Great Lakes, the Mississippi River, and the 31st degree north latitude (approximately the northern border of present-day Florida). Great Britain allowed America to fish off the coast of Newfoundland and to set up fishing camps on the beaches of Labrador and Nova Scotia. The British troops would withdraw from America, and the new government would recommend to the states that they make restitution to English sympathizers from whom they had seized property.

What did the Revolutionary War mean to the descendants of Puritans and Pilgrims, fishermen and woodsmen?

In practical terms, it meant a great financial drain. Even before the firing at Concord, normal trade had been disrupted by boycotts and blockades. By war's end, every state faced financial disaster. In order to pay their war debts, state governments were forced to impose taxes on their citizens, who were themselves facing financial ruin.

Some Americans did benefit from the war, using the wartime economy to increase their wealth. Farmers in eastern Massachusetts and along the Connecticut River were advantageously positioned to supply the Continental Army with food crops, whose prices had risen dramatically. Most farmers, however, did not produce enough surplus to supply the army. Merchants, especially in Boston, benefitted as well due to two factors. First, the Tory merchants in the city had fled, leaving behind a market that less prominent businessmen could take over. Second, when the war moved south in 1776, New York merchants were cut off from the trade

Although the British won the Battle of Bunker Hill, forcing the Continental Army to retreat after its supply of powder was gone, King George III was furious about the enormous casualties suffered by the Redcoats. Previous pages: a painting of the scene at Bunker Hill by John Trumbull.

The town of Falmouth (background), on the southern shore of Cape Cod, came under fire from the British troops on October 18, 1775, and was burned by the Redcoats under the command of Captain Moet. The city boasts a steeple bell cast by Paul Revere in the First Congregational Church.

When the battles between the British and the colonists continued, the colonists realized there was no turning back. In 1776, the Continental Congress asked Thomas Jefferson to draft a justification for the colonies' seeking of independence, and on July 4, the Congressional delegates officially adopted the Declaration of Independence, an event captured in a painting (right) by John Trumbull.

CHAPTER TWO

they had dominated, and the Bostonians picked up extra business from New York's demise.

Privateering was an activity that made many New Englanders rich. Some Massachusetts merchants took part in the dangerous business in which they captured British trade ships. In Portsmouth, New Hampshire, the state's ability to recruit volunteers for the Continental Navy had been severely jeopardized by the licensing of privateers. Here, as in Massachusetts, fortunes had been made.

The new Americans also found themselves ruled by a new form of government. In November 1777, Congress sent the Articles of Confederation to the states for ratification. Drafting a document that satisfied each delegate to Congress was no easy matter. The delegates argued over representation, the larger states wanting the number of representatives to be based on population, the smaller ones wanting one vote per state, no matter the size. Ever mindful of the trouble Parliament encountered when it attempted to tax the colonies, the delegates denied the new government the right to tax its citizens. By March 1781 all the states had ratified the Articles, which called for one vote per state and described their association as a "league of friendship." The new government was weak without the right to impose taxes or to extend its authority, and the states fought desperately to maintain their own power at the expense of the federal government. After the Articles were ratified, Congress asked the states to amend them to include the government's right to collect a five percent duty on imports. Rhode Island was adamant in refusing Congress this right. Arguing the state's case, David Howell pointed out that Rhode Island was already taxing imports in order to pay its war debts and insisted that Congress should continue to rely on voluntary contributions from the states for its revenue.

While the colonists in Massachusetts, Connecticut, Rhode Island, Maine, New Hampshire, and the other eight colonies were waging war with England, a very different kind of struggle was going on in the area known as Vermont. Throughout its

*Previous pages: G.S.
Reinhart's woodcut of the
drumming out of Tories.*

*From a belfry (left) in
Lexington, Massachusetts, the
alarm was sent to the Minute
Men to gather for action
against the Redcoats
marching from Boston in
1775. In 1797 the bell was
removed from the tower, but
in 1891 the Lexington
Historical Society returned it
to the old belfry.*

The British commander General Howe realized that the Continental Army was fortifying itself outside Boston on Dorchester Heights. Fearing another encounter resulting in casualty numbers as high as those incurred in the Battle of Bunker Hill, Howe withdrew his troops from Boston to Halifax, Nova Scotia, on March 17, 1776.

history of European settlement, the area that came to be Vermont was plagued by land disputes, which intensified in 1749 when Governor Wentworth of New Hampshire and Governor Clinton of New York began quarreling over the boundary between their two colonies. Both governors granted townships in the area, and when the Crown finally determined the boundary to be the west bank of the Connecticut River, New Hampshire was reluctant to surrender its claims. In 1770, New Yorkers filed suit against the settlers from New Hampshire. Not willing to give up their newly cleared land or to pay the fees required by New York for continued occupation, these settlers organized the Bennington Nine under the lead of Ethan Allen. After the judge at the trial in Albany refused to permit the certificates of titles Allen had brought as evidence, Allen and his attorney stormed from the courtroom. Upon his return to Bennington, Allen gathered a force of 200 men who were determined to protect the titles granted by New Hampshire.

The "Green Mountain Boys," as they called

themselves, prepared to meet the onslaught of New York surveyors coming to the area. Not content merely to prohibit the surveyors from doing their jobs, the band also expelled New Yorkers from their claims in the area. Soon the New York government declared Allen and his band outlaws and offered rewards for their capture, but the Green Mountain Boys continued their forays into the Vermont territory, preventing New York courts from sitting and New York settlers from remaining on their land. In April 1775, just a week before the firing at Lexington and Concord, a convention at Westminster petitioned King George III to allow them either to become a new colony or to annex themselves to another – other than New York. When revolution broke out, the Green Mountain Boys quickly determined the shifting tide. They captured Fort Ticonderoga, along with Benedict Arnold's troops from Connecticut, and delivered it into American hands.

The Green Mountain Boys and the Onion River Land Company, formed by four Allen brothers,

A lithograph of farmers threshing wheat in a barn during the 1780s. During the Revolutionary War, farming was an activity that had to continue. The Continental Army was always running short of food.

S.H. Gunber's engraving for Graham's Magazine *of the Battle of Cowpens shows Colonel William Augustine Washington in the midst of the conflict.*

At the Battle of Monmouth, General Washington and his troops defeated General Lee.

CHAPTER TWO

were still in limbo. Should they align themselves with New Hampshire or should they organize a new state? In January 1777, a convention meeting in Westminster declared the land formerly known as the New Hampshire Grants a separate state. Calling it at first New Connecticut, the convention at its next meeting renamed the area Vermont. By March 1778, with only some of Vermont's towns ratifying the new constitution, the first legislature was elected. The president of the independent republic of Vermont was Thomas Chittenden.

The independent republic continued to be embroiled in land disputes. First, several New Hampshire towns bordering Vermont asked the republic to incorporate them into its territory. The citizens of those towns were dissatisfied with the New Hampshire constitution that had been passed in 1776, and were hopeful that Vermont would be more responsive to their needs. Reluctant to anger New Hamsphire, but loathe to see the New Hamsphire towns follow her own recent lead in forming a new state, Vermont allowed the towns to join the republic. Massachusetts soon introduced its claims to land in southern Vermont. The Continental Congress, rightfully occupied with waging the Revolutionary War, told Massachusetts, New Hampshire, and New York to work out their differences and settle the matter of land claims in Vermont.

When Cornwallis surrendered at Yorktown, the matter was still unsettled. Early in 1779, Vermont had returned the border towns to New Hampshire, but in 1781 Vermont admitted them again, along with eighteen more. Vermont also claimed land between its western border and the Hudson River in New York. With a confrontation between Vermonters and New Yorkers narrowly avoided, the Continental Congress promised Vermont that if it gave up its claims in New Hampshire and New York, it would be admitted into the United States.

Meanwhile, the Allen brothers were pursuing some very complicated negotiations with the British – negotiations that would lead to Vermont's being named a royal province. In October 1780, Justus Sherwood came to Vermont to meet with Ethan

The *Minute Man statue (facing page) was created by Daniel Chester French. The monument stands in Concord and is a symbol of America's readiness to defend her freedom.*

Right: Ethan Allen's birthplace in Litchfield, Connecticut. Allen distinguished himself in the Revolutionary War when he and Benedict Arnold captured Fort Ticonderoga.

Allen in Castleton. Sherwood attempted to persuade Allen that the Continental Congress would not honor its promise to admit Vermont to the Union. At first, Allen would have none of it, but then he agreed to continue negotiations after extracting a promise from Sherwood that the British would cease fighting in Vermont and northern New York. At the same time, Chittenden began negotiations with Connecticut and New York suggesting that Vermont would join forces with the two colonies to repel a British invasion if New York and Connecticut would relinquish their claims to Vermont. The Allens continued their talks with the British throughout the summer. It was finally decided that when the Vermont legislature met in October, it would accept the British offer to admit Vermont into the British Empire. Two thousand British troops arrived in October at Fort Ticonderoga where they waited for word from the Allens as to when news about Vermont's joining the empire could be released. Tempers throughout Vermont flared, however, when a Vermont soldier was killed by British troops. The time was not right for announcing Vermont's reunion with Britain, so General Barry St. Leger delayed announcing the agreement. The next piece of news to reach Vermont was the surrender of Cornwallis. Now Vermonters had their answer. There was certainly no reason to reunite themselves with the British now, but the Allens, ever watchful of their land claims, kept the possibility alive.

After the war, Congress was reluctant to upset the balance between the north and south by admitting Vermont as a new northern state. As the American nation turned its attention to shoring up its new government, rivalries between the northern and southern states had emerged. When the territory of Kentucky was formed and was ready to join the Union, Congress admitted Vermont to the north and Kentucky to the south as new states, thus preserving the regional balance that became ever more important during the next eighty years. Now Vermont joined its neighbors in New England in the difficult struggle to forge their very different states into a Union.

The Battle of Cowpens, South Carolina, brought the end of the Revolutionary War in sight. Previous pages: Colonel William Augustine Washington and British Colonel Tarleton leading the fierce and lengthy conflict.

Ethan Allen (left) led the fight in Vermont to form at first a separate colony and then a separate republic. Tories were harrassed (facing page) by the American rebels throughout the new nation.

In Concord (left), the Redcoats destroyed the military supplies of the colonial forces and started on their way back to Boston. colonial snipers plagued their return march; at the end of the day, 273 British troops were dead. John Trumbull's M'Fingal: A Modern Epic Poem (below left) depicted the demise of Tories, people who remained loyal to England during the Revolutionary War.

TORY'S DAY of JUDGEMENT.

M'FINGAL:

A MODERN

EPIC POEM

IN

FOUR CANTOS.

BY JOHN TRUMBULL, ESQ.

EMBELLISHED WITH PLATES.

WITH

EXPLANATORY NOTES.

BALTIMORE.
PRINTED AND SOLD BY A. ALTENBERGER,
No. 10, North Howard Street.

1812

THE PROCESSION.

Background: the Green Mountain Boys in council. During such meetings, the army planned raids on settlers with New York land grants. In January 1777, a convention meeting in Westminster declared that the New Hampshire grants were thereafter to mark a separate state. Captain Samuel Nicholas recruited American men for the First Continental Marines, whose uniforms and accoutrements were detailed in an engraving (far right).

STATEHOOD AND THE NEW ENGLAND FEDERALISTS

John Hancock (facing page) (1737-1793) was elected the first governor of the new state of Massachusetts in 1780. He had built his reputation among voters by serving as president of the Continental Congress. He held the governor's seat in Massachusetts for most of the years beginning in 1780 until his death.

While the Continental Congress struggled to create a new central government under the Articles of Confederation, the colonies renounced their dependence on the mother country and set about establishing state governments. In the New England states, citizens voted to operate in much the same way as they had before, under constitutions in some cases based on their old royal charters. But the transition from royal colony to independent state was not easy. Massachusetts suffered under rebellions led by Daniel Shays who represented the interests of small farmers against the wealthy merchants. Rhode Island was the target of attacks by other states when its legislature continued to issue paper money that was nearly worthless. Under the Articles of Confederation, there was little that the federal government could do to quell rebellions such as Shays' or to force Rhode Island to conform to its neighbors' economic policies.

When delegates to a convention in Philadelphia drew up a new federal constitution, old fears about

Right: a Maynard painting captured the essence of the young country.

117

the dangers of a strong central government were aroused in New England. Pro-Constitution Federalists argued that a strong government was needed to effect economic stability and to come to the aid of states suffering under rebellions. Anti-federalists believed that the new constitution would destroy the independence of the states.

Once the states ratified the Constitution, New Englanders saw a new kind of danger in the person of Thomas Jefferson. Backed by the new Democratic Republican Party, Jefferson won the presidential election of 1800. The New Englanders' Puritan heritage came to bear as they focused sharp attacks on the Deist Jefferson. Additionally, they were adamant in fighting against Jefferson's Louisiana Purchase, declaring that the federal government had no right to extend America's borders in such a way and fearing that the newly expanded West and the South would join forces to reduce New England's power in Congress.

Great Britain and France had gone to war in 1795, and New Englanders feared that America was nearing a decision to join the fray. Merchants suffered attacks on their ships by both France and Great Britain, and the British impressed American crewmen. But these attacks were preferable to war, which New Englanders believed would adversely affect their business. The War Hawks in Congress, determined to repay Britain for the indignities she had showered on the new American nation, were successful in pushing America into the War of 1812.

The New England states established governments that were relatively similar to each other. Each new state called for the election of a legislature and an executive, or governor. A system of courts and judges was also established in each state, but the power of the judges and the governor was limited. The legislatures were most powerful in these fledgling states. Not only could they pass laws, they could also declare war, carry out foreign relations, and control the courts. Bills of rights were included in the new state constitutions to protect the citizens against oppressive action by the legislature or the executive.

New Hampshire officially changed its status

Previous pages: George Washington presiding over the Continental Congress in Philadelphia in 1787. Under the Articles of Confederation, the new Federal Government of the United States was weak. In 1786, however, delegates to a constitutional convention started work to strengthen it. They threw out the Articles of Confederation and put in its place a new Constitution that gave the central government much more power than it had had before.

A Currier and Ives lithograph (left) embodied the Spirit of '76 in a thoughtful young man ready to fight for his freedom.

from colony to state on September 11, 1776. Earlier that year, the Fifth Provincial Congress of New Hampshire had redesigned its workings – forming a House of Representatives and creating another body called the Council. Eighty-nine representatives from five counties composed the House, and the number of representatives each county had was determined by the size of its population. The Council of twelve men was chosen by the House. As the first to establish a state government, New Hampshire was acting on need. When the royal governor John Wentworth had fled the colony before hostilities broke out, he left New Hampshire without a government.

The new legislature took immediate action to ease the transition from colony to state. Abolishing the court of appeals in order to forestall any attempts by citizens to appeal to Great Britain, the legislators then undertook a thorough review of all laws on the books. Some were repealed; others were reaffirmed.

The constitution in New Hampshire underwent a series of revisions between 1776 and 1784. During the debates over the constitution, western New Hampshirites fought bitterly for the elimination of voting restrictions, and although such restrictions, based on property, were not abandoned altogether, they were reduced. The New Hampshire legislators had been forced to listen to their constituencies from the west: indeed, had they not, the towns along the bank of the Connecticut River might have remained permanently a part of Vermont. The 1784 constitution called for three independent branches – legislative, executive, and judicial – and it included a bill of rights.

In Connecticut, the general assembly did not draft a new constitution until 1818. Choosing to base its authority on Connecticut's charter of 1662, the general assembly simply adopted a resolution in October 1776 that called for the dropping from the charter of all references to Great Britain. Rhode Island, too, merely adopted a resolution declaring the colony to be a state. Roger Williams' charter was altered in one way: the word "state" was substituted for the word "colony."

Massachusetts started along its road to statehood in the summer of 1776, when the courts that had been closed by the Administration of Justice Act were reopened. But the framing of a constitution was another matter. The general court was not able to persuade the citizens of the need to pass a new governing document until 1780.

In 1776, the general court first asked citizens to vote on whether Massachusetts should have a new constitution in 1776. The vote was "No". Two years later, the House of Representatives drafted a document, but it too was rejected. Debate over its passage focused on several issues: some felt that the office of the governor was too weak; others disputed the property-holding requirements for senators and governors. Representation, though, was a central issue. Citizens of the more heavily populated east were dismayed that the document called for one representative from each town, regardless of its population.

The next attempt at drafting a constitution was in the spring of 1779 when voters approved a constitutional convention. Revolutionary leaders, such as John and Samuel Adams and John Hancock, were among the delegates to the convention meeting in September of that year. The delegates appointed John Adams to the task of drafting the document. In his work Adams included a bill of rights stipulating the protection of citizens from oppression by the government, a free press, the right to assembly, and the right to keep and bear arms. He also included some provisions aimed directly at avoiding the type of government oppression Massachusetts had suffered under the hands of Parliament; specifically prohibited was the right of government to confiscate property for use in housing military troops, a right that Great Britain had claimed through its Quartering Act.

A modicum of religious tolerance was introduced into Massachusetts in the constitution. Calling for the support of churches by taxation, the constitution stipulated that taxes raised from individuals would be paid directly to the church of their choice. If no church were specified, however, the funds would be paid to the largest denomination in the individuals' towns. That the Congregational Church was not the sole recipient of tax revenue was new to residents of the state.

In terms of representation, Massachusetts' constitution called for two legislative bodies. The senate would include representatives, elected annually, from tax districts that were equal in size. The lower house included one representative from each incorporated town. Governors, senators, representatives, and even voters themselves had to meet property qualifications of various levels.

After the ratification of the state constitution in 1780, voters elected John Hancock governor. Hancock had become well known, not only in Massachusetts but in other colonies as well through his roles as president of the Provincial Congress, chairman of the Committee of Safety, and then president of the Continental Congress. He held the governorship for most of the years between 1780 and his death in 1793. In 1785, when Massachusetts faced a financial crisis over taxation, he retired briefly from the governorship.

Despite the relative ease with which New Englanders adopted constitutions, trouble was brewing throughout the land over war debts and taxation. Faced with an overwhelming war debt, Hancock's successor in Massachusetts, James Bowdoin, decided that taxes should be raised. Farmers, already in dire straits due to falling farm prices, organized themselves into an army of resistance, with Daniel Shays and Luke Day as leaders. At a convention in Hatfield, in August 1786, representatives of fifty towns adopted a long list of grievances against the state government. The delegates objected to court fees, apportionment, the system of taxation, the government's refusal to issue paper money, and the location of the general court in Boston. Immediately after the convention, a thousand armed men marched on Northampton where they occupied the courthouse. After a similar incident in Worcester, Governor Bowdoin ordered the state militia to occupy the courthouse in Springfield. Nevertheless, Shay's army managed to force the court to close.

Shays called for another convention in Hampshire. Alarmed at the news that the convention was urging towns to prepare for war, the Massachusetts legislature passed a riot act and suspended the right of habeas corpus. In an attempt to quell the rebellion, the legislature passed relief acts and offered amnesty to all rebels who would take an oath of allegiance to the state by January 1, 1787. Despite these modest strides towards reconciliation, the rebellion continued through the fall and early winter. By calling out the entire militia, the government opened the courts in Worcester, but it was unable to prevent the spilling of blood later in Springfield.

The arsenal in Springfield was held by 900 militiamen. Shays, though, had a force of 2,000 at hand. On January 25, Shays' army marched on the arsenal, ignoring threats of fire by the militia. At first, the troops fired over the rebels' heads, but still the determined army marched on. When the militia fired cannons directly at the Shaysites, they were routed. By week's end, the rebels had had enough, and they requested a pardon from the state. The time for pardon, however, was passed. Since Shays' men were still in arms, the government sent the militia to overtake them in Petersham. The surprise attack ended with Shays' escape across the state line and the rebels being disarmed and sent home.

Shays' Rebellion brought into dramatic view the need for a stronger central government. Under the weak Articles of Confederation, the federal government could do nothing to aid Massachusetts in supressing the rebellion. In Rhode Island, another incident pointed to the need for a stronger central government – and this incident was not begun by rebellious citizens but by the government itself.

Since 1710 Rhode Island had persisted in a practice that earned its citizens disdain from their neighbors: the issuing of paper money. During Queen Anne's War, the government was unable to collect taxes from citizens. The solution adopted was to issue bills of credit that would remain valid until the stringent circumstances of the war were alleviated. While the colony did not stop issuing bills of credit after the war, those put into

Delegates to the Massachusetts Constitutional Convention selected John Adams (1735-1826) as the principal writer of the new state document. His work became a model for other states and for the delegates to the Philadelphia convention that wrote a new constitution for the United States in 1786. Adams was elected Vice President of the United States in 1789 and President in 1796.

circulation after 1714 were based on land. Holders of these bills of credit could use them as though they were gold or silver, but they were subjected to yearly interest payments, and holders of the bills were required to pay them off within ten years. The government found the paper money so useful that it soon abandoned its plan to retire the amount of paper paid off each year, and instead it issued more and more. By 1738, more than 3384,000 of paper bills were in circulation.

The government was reluctant to retire the bills because their use had created a boom economy. Acceptable in most New England colonies, though not in England, the money boosted production, trade, and sales. But because the government did not retire the bills, they lost value, becoming worth only half their face value by 1750.

At the end of the Revolutionary War, Rhode Island persisted in its paper money policy, even though other colonies were returning to a hard-money basis. To retire its own war debts, Rhode Island needed taxes, which the poor farmers in the state were unable to pay. As a solution to the problem, the legislature approved a land-bank system similar to the one instituted in 1710. Jonathan J. Hazard, Daniel Owen, and John Collins, leaders of the "Country Party" in control of Rhode Island from 1785 to 1790, also proposed that Rhode Island be free of responsibility for the loan certificates and promissory notes the Continental Congress had issued to people in the state. Since Congress had no power to tax individuals under the Articles of Confederation, it could not honor its debts, and the notes it had in circulation lost value. Citizens in the state soon divided over the issue. The wealthy citizens of Newport, Portsmouth, Middletown, and elsewhere wanted to adopt Congress's proposal to accept the notes they held. The Country Party believed that Rhode Island had a better chance of paying off its debts under the state's own financial system. These individuals wanted to go it alone; thus they opposed the ratification of the Constitution which would give Congress the right to tax citizens.

The Country Party attempted to force the

Previous pages: John Hancock's mansion on Beacon Street in Boston. Hancock inherited this house from his uncle Thomas Hancock, who began his career as a bookseller and later became well versed in the art of smuggling imported dry goods, tea and cutlery past the Crown's customs officials.

When Governor James Bowdoin raised taxes in Massachusetts, poor, angry farmers organized an army of resistance (left) under Daniel Shays and Luke Day. Shays and his followers seized the courthouse in Northampton in 1786, so the Governor ordered out the state militia.

acceptance of paper money. Creditors who would not accept paper for debts were fined and were prohibited from voting. Rather than being forced into accepting paper money that had little of its original value, many creditors fled the state. In the case of *Trevett v. Weeden*, the court overturned the law. (The court that heard the case has the distinction of being the first American court to overturn an act by a legislature.) But although the fines and disenfranchisement stipulations attached to the law were repealed, the requirement of accepting paper money remained on the books. The law also allowed debtors to pay their creditors in an unusual way. Debtors could give a local judge the amount of money owed, and if the creditor did not claim it, the debt was cancelled.

Not only was a strong central government needed to assert control in rebellions such as Shays', it was also needed to introduce economic stability and monetary standards. Reforms to the central government began in January 1786 when the Virginia legislature issued a call for a convention of all the states to discuss commerce. Only five delegates came to the meeting held in September of that year in Annapolis. Not content to give up so easily, Alexander Hamilton of New York called another convention for the next spring in Philadelphia. Delegates from all the states, except Rhode Island, where feelings for the need for independence were still strong, met for four months with George Washington as president of the convention.

The twenty-nine delegates were nearly unanimous in their belief that a stronger federal government was needed. Also widespread among the delegates was the desire for a republican form of government. Originally charged with redrafting the Articles of Confederation, the delegates soon realized that a whole new framework was needed. After voting to establish a national government, the delegates then assigned to the new government the right to levy taxes. The delegates also assigned the duty of regulating interstate and foreign commerce to the government. In reaction to Shays' Rebellion, the delegates gave the central government the right

The Continental Congress issued paper bills during the war. Top right: a thirty-dollar note issued by the Continental Congress in 1779. Above right: a fifty-dollar note, front and back, also issued in 1779. Right: a note declaring its value at forty dollars. Americans soon came to say that something that had no value was "not worth a Continental."

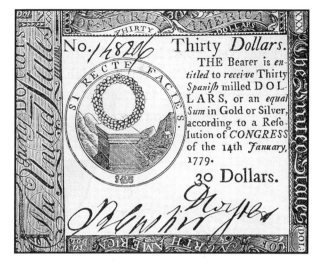

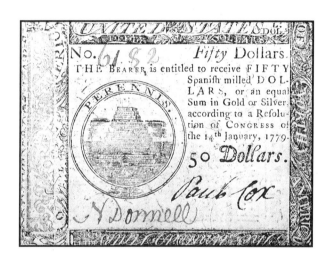

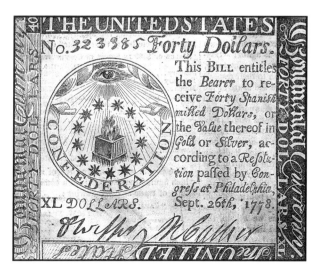

CHAPTER THREE

In 1785, John Hancock retired briefly from the governorship of Massachusetts. His successor, James Bowdoin, was left with huge state war debts to pay, which was why he decided to raise taxes.

A Massachusetts Treasury note dated August 18, 1775. Its inscription reads "Issued in Defense of American Liberty." Throughout the Revolutionary War years, the new states all issued paper money.

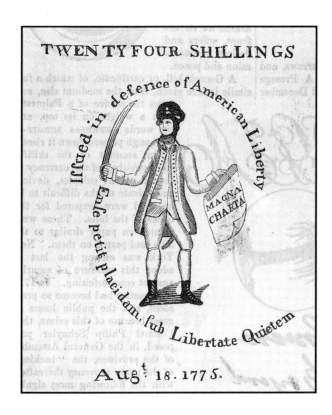

representatives each state would have in the House. Another compromise, called the "Three-Fifths Compromise," determined that "three-fifths of all other Persons" would be counted in determining both taxes and representation.

The new constitution called for the election of an executive branch – a president and vice-president – and for the establishment of federal courts. The powers of the president were dramatically increased in the new constitution. Presidential duties consisted of serving as Commander-in-Chief of the armed forces, supervisor of all foreign affairs, and appointer of federal judges. Additionally, the president could veto any law passed by Congress, although the legislature did retain the power to overrule a presidential veto with a two-thirds majority in both the House and the Senate.

After the constitution was approved by the convention on September 17, the framers decided that each state should call a convention of delegates to ratify the document. Feelings were mixed among the population at large. Those in favor of ratification were called "Federalists"; those opposed, "Anti-federalists." In very general terms, Federalists were professional men of some wealth and were active in commerce. The Anti-federalist group, generally, consisted of small farmers. The most prevalent fear voiced by the Anti-federalists was that the new constitution would weaken the authority of the states to such a degree that they would no longer be independent. To allay these fears, the delegates decided to add amendments to the constitution.

New Hampshire delegates John Langdon and Nicholas Gilman were in favor of a strong central government, but during their absence from the state, a strong opposing force had developed. When the convention in Exeter seemed likely to vote against ratification, Federalist leaders managed to persuade delegates to vote for an adjournment. When the meeting reconvened in June 1788, delegates voted 57 to 46 in favor of ratification.

In Connecticut, a conflict brewing between merchants and farmers came to a head during meetings to discuss the new central government.

to raise an army and navy and to call out state militia for the purpose of enforcing national laws and suppressing rebellions. And, in reaction to Rhode Island's fiscal policies, the delegates withdrew the states' right to issue paper money. Additionally, the states were forbidden to make treaties or to tax imports and exports without approval from Congress.

The issue of representation was central to the debate at the convention. Larger states wanted representation to be based on population size; smaller ones wanted each state to have one vote. Roger Sherman of Connecticut proposed a compromise that resulted in the formation of a new legislature whose lower house would be based on population and whose upper house would have two members from each state.

Slavery, too, was hotly debated. The northern states wanted slaves to be counted in determining each state's federal taxes; the southern states did not want to count slaves for tax purposes but did want to count them for deciding the number of

Shay's Rebellion was finally crushed in January 1787. The uprising was one of several events that brought into dramatic relief the need for a stronger central government that could help the various states in times of crisis.

Merchants in the state had prospered during the Revolutionary War, trading with the French and Danish in the Caribbean, becoming privateers, and supplying the state and national commissaries. Farmers, on the other hand, had fared badly. Small farmers, who were much more prevalent than large ones, were unable to produce large enough surpluses to sell to the state militia or Continental Army. They had also been hard hit by Connecticut's tax system which was based on real property. Although Connecticut altered the tax base during the war to cover business profits in addition to land, the small farmers remained bitter and suspicious of wealthy merchants. At a convention in Middletown in September 1783, they made clear that they would not stand for a stronger central government whose authority included taxation. But Connecticut's Federalists ultimately had their way. At the convention in Hartford, delegates voted 128 to 40 in favor of ratification.

In Massachusetts, too, where memories of Shays' Rebellion were so raw, the conflict over ratification pitted farmers against merchants and manufacturers. At the convention in 1788, opponents voiced fears over the central government's right to tax, over the length of terms of elected officials, and over the omission of religious requirements for officials. At the beginning of the convention, those opposed to ratification held a majority, but under the capable leadership of Samuel Adams and Governor John Hancock, the Federalists were successful in swaying the majority to vote for ratification.

By the end of June 1788, only Rhode Island, New York, and North Carolina had not ratified the Constitution, but even without these states, the new Constitution was in force – with New Hampshire serving as the ninth and final state needed for ratification.

The Rhode Island legislature, controlled by the Country Party, voted thirteen times between 1787 and 1789 to oppose the convening of a constitutional convention. In Congress, political leaders were horrified by the state's position. Congress threatened to divide the tiny state between its neighbors and to impose duties on exports from Rhode Island to other states. By 1790, though, the Country Party had fallen from power, and Rhode Islanders were eager to receive the payments for war debts promised by Congress. In town meetings in Providence, Newport, Middletown, Portsmouth, and Bristol, citizens voted for ratification, and by May 1790, the delegates to the constitutional convention voted 34 to 32 in favor. Rhode Island was the last of the original thirteen colonies to ratify the Constitution.

In January and February 1789, the states held elections for president and vice-president. On April 6, the Senate counted the ballots confirming George Washington as the unanimous choice for president and John Adams as his vice-president.

Congress then set about fulfilling the promise made by the Constitutional Convention for amendments. The Bill of Rights consisted of ten amendments guaranteeing freedom of speech, the press, and religion, trial by jury, and freedom from unreasonable searches and seizures. The amendments also prohibited courts from requiring an individual to testify against himself and prohibited individuals from being "deprived of life, liberty, or property, without due process of law."

While America struggled to enforce the Constitution and to overcome her war debts, Great Britain and France went to war in 1795. Although President Washington issued a statement of neutrality, the French Government sent Edmond Charles Genet to the United States to generate support for the French cause. He set about licensing American ships as privateers against the British and granting military commissions to Americans who would lead attacks against the Spanish and British holdings in North America. Although Washington ordered Genet to stop these illegal activities, he continued, and eventually Washington demanded that the French Government recall him from America.

Now, not only did Great Britain capture American ships engaged in trade; France did as well. As many as 600 American vessels were seized in 1793 and 1794. Old hatreds of the British surfaced throughout the commercial shipping

CHAPTER THREE

industry. Washington sent Chief Justice John Jay to Great Britain to try to negotiate a treaty. Jay was able to extract from the British some major concessions: a promise to abandon British forts in the West, to compensate American shipowners for their losses, and to allow American ships to trade in British colonies in Asia. Some clauses in the treaty angered New Englanders. They did not want to grant "most-favored nation" status to Great Britain, nor did they want to be held to payments of pre-Revolutionary war debts owed to British merchants. Although it was condemned as pro-British throughout the country, the treaty was finally passed by Congress, at Washington's urging, on June 24, 1795. In the long-run, the treaty instituted a long process of regularizing relations between America and Great Britain, and it unexpectedly brought about a new period of expansion in the American southwest. Afraid that Britain might attack her North American holdings and that the new Jay Treaty would result in cooperation of the Americans in such attacks, Spain signed a treaty negotiated by Thomas Pinckney that gave the United States navigation rights in the Mississippi River and the right to use the port of New Orleans. With these two treaties, American territory was extended beyond the Appalachian Mountains to the Mississippi River.

The debate over the ratification of the Constitution and the dividing of Americans over the war between France and England aided in the formation of distinct political parties. The pro-Constitution Federalists had strong leaders in John Adams and Alexander Hamilton. With the recent victory of ratification still in their minds, the Federalists held power in the presidential election of 1796, with John Adams of Massachusetts becoming the second United States president.

Opposition to the Federalists coalesced around Thomas Jefferson and James Madison of Virginia. Jefferson had been elected vice-president in 1796. A believer in the intrinsic evil of any form of government, Jefferson hoped for an idealized society of small independent farmers. He feared that Hamilton's economic plans would promote the

Despite attempts by the Federal Government to halt or at least curtail trade with the British in Canada during the years before the War of 1812, smuggling activities flourished. Previous pages: a sketch by J. Becker shows government officials watching as a smuggling boat from New Brunswick nears the shore in Calais, Maine.

To President Thomas Jefferson, American farmers (left) were the image of hope for America's future. He envisioned a country peopled by farmers and their families, each working its own parcel of land and sharing responsibility for America's destiny. Background: a ten-dollar note issued as part of a land bank system.

growth of cities, which would ultimately require more governmental controls. Just as the proponents in the constitution debate did not fall into distinct class divisions, the line between the Federalists and Jefferson's Democratic Republicans was murky. Federalists tended to be merchants, manufacturers, and farmers whose surpluses were great enough to allow them to carry on trade. Democratic Republicans tended to be small farmers and frontiersmen. The first crises of John Adams' presidency sharpened the rhetoric, if not the distinction, between the parties.

The crisis arose when the French stepped up their attacks on American shipping after the Jay Treaty went into effect. Adams sent three commissioners to negotiate with the French. The French foreign minister also sent three commissioners. These three Frenchmen, who were soon called "X, Y, and Z," were instructed to extract a payment from the Americans in return for France's promise to stop capturing American ships. After the Americans refused to pay the bribe and President Adams issued the commissioners' report, the American population was outraged.

Federalists in Congress thought the time was right to quell opposition by the Democratic Republicans, who in general favored strengthening relations with France rather than with Great Britain. Congress passed a series of laws called the Alien and Sedition Acts. The Naturalization Law, aimed at controlling the influx of immigrants from Revolutionary France, raised the number of years of residence required by foreigners before they could become citizens. The Alien Enemies Act authorized the President to deport aliens during times of declared war. The Alien Act allowed the President to deport all aliens dangerous to the United States. The Sedition Act declared it illegal to block the enforcement of any law and to publish or make "false, scandalous and malicious" remarks about the government. Democratic Republicans rallied behind Jefferson and Madison in their criticism of the Sedition Act, declaring it an abrogation of their right

to a free press and freedom of speech.

The furor soon died down when the French declared that they would be open to new negotiations – this time without the imposition of a bribe. But the Federalists, in their attempts to smother dissent at any cost, had lost support. In the election of 1800, Thomas Jefferson and Aaron Burr were elected president and vice-president.

In Massachusetts, the election brought to bitter debate not only the differences between the political parties but also those between the candidates themselves. Massachusetts citizens were horrified that Jefferson, a Deist and Francophile, might win the election, but there was little that the aging John Adams, the incumbent Federalist candidate, could do. When the voters put Jefferson in office, Massachusetts Federalists became ever more determined to preserve a local stronghold that maintained the religious establishment and promoted the interests of commerce and manufacturing. Organizing themselves for local elections, they created Washington Benevolent Societies, membership organizations that espoused Federalists views. Throughout the state, thousands of people joined these groups and participated in local debates.

Federalists had been in control of the political life of the nation since the end of the Revolution. Their legacies included a strong central government, successful negotiations with the British in the form of the Jay Treaty, workable fiscal policies, and a diversified economy. Their defeat was brought about in part by their inflexibility. They were unable to change their positions regarding the careful monitoring of political participation by the common man. They placed the goal of achieving an efficient, orderly government above that of protecting and promoting individual freedom. Their losses in 1800 were not only on the national level but on the state and local level as well.

New Hampshire's Federalists Party had run the affairs of the state since the beginning and was especially dominant in the seacoast towns. Before

CHAPTER THREE

the election, the Federalist government made a fatal mistake: it closed a bank that had been created to issue loans on easy terms. Democratic Republicans called the action a direct assault on the common man. The Democratic Republican candidate for governor won the election, and the Federalist majority in the legislature was severely cut.

The splintered nature of American politics vexed President Jefferson as he tried to deal with the repercussions of renewed hostilities between France and Britain. American shipowners had prospered at the beginning of the war, but when France and Great Britain waged commercial warfare, Americans were hurt. Napoleon declared all commerce with Great Britain illegal. Great Britain blockaded most ports on the European continent and required ships bound for those ports to sail first to England and pay customs duties. Also, there was the matter of impressment. Great Britain had a standing policy of drafting her subjects during times of emergencies. Normally such drafts occurred in British ports, but if a British ship in need of men was away from home, the ship's captain would stop neutral ships and draft any British subjects on board. Paying no heed to America's naturalization laws, the British Government in this way impressed 5,000 sailors between 1803 and 1812, with an estimated 75 percent being Americans. The issue of impressment forced Jefferson to act. Striving to avoid war, even after the American ship *Chesapeake* was fired on by the British ship *Leopard*, Jefferson pushed the Embargo Act through Congress.

Now New England shipowners, merchants, and manufacturers felt directly the effects of war. Exportation of American goods came to an end. Prices of crops and manufactured good plummeted. In Portland, Maine, unemployed citizens were fed in soup kitchens, and throughout the seacoast towns, widespread unemployment existed. In some cases nearly sixty percent of the population was out of work. In Connecticut, Democratic Republicans lost seats in the lower house of the general assembly, their representation falling to thirty-six seats. Throughout America, merchants attempted to circumvent the hated embargo. Vermonters and

CHAPTER THREE

Mainers continued their prosperous trade with Canada; some even sent naval supplies to the Isle aux Noix and St. John where the British had shipyards.

Finally, during the last week of Jefferson's administration, Congress repealed the Embargo Act and replaced it with the Non-Intercourse Act. Much more palatable to American traders, the new act did not forbid all trade – only trade with France and Great Britain. For citizens in Vermont, New Hampshire, and Maine, however, the Non-Intercourse Act still outlawed their valuable trade with Canada and so they persisted in smuggling goods back and forth across the border.

Tensions over the blockades and impressment mounted, however, and added to them were cries from westerners that the British were aiding the Indians in their attempts to expel American settlers. Under the new Commander-in-Chief and President, James Madison, the American navy, with the aid of several hundred privateers, set out to destroy the largest navy in the world. But Madison had little help from the New England states during the War of 1812. The governors of Connecticut, Rhode Island, and Massachusetts declared that they would not provide troops for America's war effort. Nevertheless, America was successful in her first attacks on the British. Despite the declaration of non-cooperation, Rhode Island did provide five hundred troops to the United States Army, and one Rhode Islander became a national hero. Oliver Hazard Perry, from South Kingstown, re-entered the navy at the beginning of the war. Ordered to rid the Great Lakes of British forces, he went to Sacketts Harbor on Lake Erie where he took command of a fleet of ten ships. At Put-In Bay, Perry encountered the British fleet of warships and eventually forced the British to surrender. To General William Henry Harrison, Perry sent the message that has since been so widely quoted: "We have met the enemy and they are ours."

Perry's victory notwithstanding, the American navy soon faltered. British forces captured the islands in Passamaquoddy Bay, Maine, and then moved on to Castine, and Bangor. By the fall of 1814, all of Maine east of the Penobscot River was in British hands. This occupation caused a shift in attitudes among Mainers. Before their land was actually occupied, they had condemned the federal government for warmongering. But now, matters were much more serious, and Mainers were losing their property through confiscation and destruction by the British troops.

Attacks on Connecticut, however, did little to alter public opinion. In April 1814, two hundred British sailors destroyed twenty American ships at Pettipaug Point (Essex), and in August of that year, the British bombarded the town of Stonington for two days. But still Connecticut remained bitter about the American policy that brought the country to war.

In the west, the American army faced extreme difficulty in trying to keep the British out of Ohio. The British devised a three-pronged attack to defeat the Americans. Eleven thousand troops would march south from Montreal; another force would attack Washington and Baltimore; and yet another would attack New Orleans. While the British were successful in invading Washington, where they burned the White House and other public buildings, the attack on Baltimore failed. In New Orleans, the Americans forced the British to retreat in a battle that left 2,100 British casualties. The battle need never have taken place. By December 1814, when it occurred, the British and Americans had already agreed to the terms of the Treaty of Ghent, restoring relations and possessions to their pre-war status.

Another incident need not have happened – this one far away from New Orleans back in Hartford, Connecticut. In December 1814, a group of Federalists met to protest the war and to plan a convention to revise the Constitution. New Englanders had opposed the war from the beginning. They had preferred the indignity of impressment and the inconvenience of running blockades to Jefferson's embargo. Some of the delegates at the meeting favored New England's seceding from the Union and forming a New England Confederacy. Fortunately for the infant

In 1812, America went to war with Great Britain once again, this time to defend American naval rights and to end the impressment of American citizens into the British navy. Previous pages: a painting depicting the battle between the Bon Homme Richard *and the British frigate* Serapis.

During the War of 1812, British troops stormed Washington, D.C., where they burned government buildings. Right: Dolly Madison saving the Declaration of Independence from the flames.

country preoccupied with warring against England for the second time in less than half a century, moderate Federalists swayed the delegates toward proposing a series of constitutional amendments. One required a two-thirds majority in Congress before war could be declared. Another prohibited presidents from the same state succeeding each other. All this was moot. News of the Treaty of Ghent and the American victory at New Orleans reached the delegates, and the Federalist Party was all but finished.

The Democratic Republicans in Connecticut took great advantage of the controversy. Accusing the Federalists of unpatriotic behavior, the party won in election after election. By 1817, the Federalists had lost control of the lower house of the legislature, and the governorship. The time was then ripe to draft a new Constitution. This effected a separation of Church and State that had never existed in Connecticut before. The Congregational Church, for years supported by taxes imposed on members and nonmembers of the church alike, would no longer be the official church of the state. The new Constitution also ushered in broader political participation, established annual elections and sessions of the legislature, and gave more power to the office of the governor and to the courts.

Change was in the wind in New Hampshire as well. With the increasing strength of the Democratic Republican Party after the 1800 election, the legislature passed laws that provided more freedom and protection to its citizens. In 1819, the legislature untied the official bond between the Congregationalist Church and the state. Additionally, the humanitarian legislators outlawed debtors' prisons and passed laws regulating child labor and factory hours and providing for the care of the insane.

Democratic Republicans carried the presidential election of 1816 with their candidate James Monroe of Virginia. The new president attempted to pacify the defeated Federalists by visiting their stronghold

By the 1820s, Daniel Webster (left) from New Hampshire had become a first-rate constitutional lawyer in Boston and was viewed as one of New England's up-and-coming political leaders. He was also a formidable orator, eloquently and vehemently opposed to high tariffs on behalf of his New England constituents, who feared the tariffs would raise the prices of the imported raw materials they needed for manufacturing. However, Webster and the New Englanders soon realized that protective measures were needed, and the "Tariff of Abominations" became law. Background: a woodcut depicting Boston citizens welcoming Webster to the city.

in New England on a good-will tour, and he was greeted by enthusiastic crowds, especially in Boston, where a Federalist newspaperman proclaimed the age an "Era of Good Feelings."

Monroe wisely brought together people whose political differences were extreme. His administration, while grounded in Democratic Republican policies, advanced the old Federalist cause as well. He retained much of the Federalists' economic policies, passed a protective tariff favorable to American manufacturing, and authorized bills for federal assistance to the states' transportation projects. One issue that continued to be hotly debated was slavery and its expansion into the territory Jefferson had bought from France in the Louisiana Purchase. Tied to the issue was that of independence for Maine.

Citizens in Maine clamored for independence from Massachusetts as a result of the Bay State's poor defense of its northern territory. Money raised for Massachusetts' defense during the war was spent on defending Boston. Under occupation by British troops, Maine received little help. The Democratic Republicans talked about secession during December 1814, but when the British were defeated and left the area, the impetus for independence died down. Such talk was not new, however. It came to the forefront immediately after the Revolutionary War and centered on the differences between Maine and Massachusetts. But Shays' Rebellion in Massachusetts quelled the interests of the prospective secessionists. In 1800 the Democratic Republicans picked up the charge, and under the leadership of William King of Bath, they tried to sway public opinion toward separation from the Federalist-dominated government of Massachusetts. At the end of the War of 1812, Maine citizens voted 10,391 to 6,501 in favor of separation. Although only a small minority of eligible voters participated in the referendum, the general court scheduled a constitutional convention for September 1816. When the issue of separation was put to a vote again, the margin of approval was

slim – 11,969 to 10,347, far short of the five to four majority stipulated by the general court for approval. For the next three years, the Democratic Republicans worked hard to buttress their cause, and when another referendum was held in July 1819, the vote was 17,091 to 7,132 in favor of separation. That fall, delegates to a convention in Portland drafted a constitution that included total religious freedom and universal adult male suffrage. The constitution did not impose religious or property restrictions on those serving as governor.

The next hurdle for Maine was gaining admission to the Union. Months before the bill on Maine statehood reached Congress, a similar bill for Missouri had been introduced. Attached to the Missouri bill was an amendment by New York Representative James Tallmadge prohibiting any future importing of slaves into Missouri and calling for the manumission, at the age of twenty-five, of all slaves born in the state . The amendment passed the House, but was rejected in the Senate.

When the bill for Maine's statehood was attached to the bill for Missouri's statehood, Maine citizens faced a moral crisis. While they avidly wanted independence, they were loathe to be a party to the spread of slavery. Even those who had worked hardest promoting statehood contemplated the withdrawal of the bill. When Congress met in 1820 for its next session, northerners and southerners reached a compromise that put Maine directly in the middle. Missouri would be allowed into the Union as a slave state, and Maine would enter as a nonslave state. Thereafter, the Missouri Compromise prohibited slavery in all territories north of 36° 30' north latitude – Missouri's southern border. But this dilemma, in which a freedom-loving New England state had to choose between the furthering of slavery elsewhere and its own dependence on an increasingly alien government was only one of many that New Englanders would face during the nineteenth century.

The long succession of Virginian presidents ended after James Monroe. Jefferson, Madison, and

Monroe had all introduced into the American political scene a degree of democracy not seen before. More and more politicians were swayed to the Democratic Republican side – even the son of John Adams, the staunchest Federalist of them all. When John Quincy Adams, who started his political career as a Federalist senator from Massachusetts in 1803, became the nation's sixth president in 1824, he did so as a Democratic Republican.

The debate that surrounded the presidential election focused on the personalities of the candidates themselves and on sectional differences. William H. Crawford and John C. Calhoun represented the southern interests – states' rights; low, or no, tariffs; high prices for western lands; and the freedom for new states to determine whether they would be slave-holding or free. Henry Clay and Andrew Jackson represented the western interests, which were new to the political scene. Westerners wanted protective tariffs that would ensure that their modest harvests would find ready markets in the east. They also wanted the government to sell western lands at very low prices. In the matter of slavery they tended to favor the southern position. The north, represented by John Quincy Adams and Daniel Webster, favored protective tariffs, despite many New Englanders' initial opposition to such measures rooted in the fact that their economy was based heavily on shipping. Northerners sided with the southerners in their desire for the American government to earn much-needed cash from the sale of western lands.

John Quincy Adams had served as secretary of state under Monroe and had been heavily involved in the formation of the Monroe Doctrine, which declared the intention of America to block any further colonization in the American continents by European powers. A strong nationalist, Adams supported the creation of a national bank and favored federal aid to the states for the building of road and canals. Daniel Webster from New Hampshire was a first-rate constitutional lawyer practicing in Boston in the 1820s. With formidable oratory skills, he opposed high tariffs, the national bank, federal participation in road and canal

Previous pages: Daniel Webster after a painting by Healy. Webster sometimes used the oratory skills for which he was well known to support causes unpopular in New England. In March 1850, he completely alienated his New England supporters by backing the Compromise of 1850. He died in 1852, only a few months after his unsuccessful attempt to win the Whig Party's nomination for the presidency.

By the time Andrew Jackson was elected president in 1828, dandies (left) shared responsibility for shaping America's future with others who were less wealthy. The country was a democracy where more than just a privileged few enjoyed full participation in government.

building, and cheap land.

In the election, the Electoral College cast 99 votes for Jackson, 84 for Adams, 41 for Crawford, and 37 for Clay. (Calhoun had previously declared himself for the vice-presidency, which he won convincingly.) Since there was no majority among the votes, the election, by constitutional law, was thrown to the House of Representatives. Clay managed to swing his support to Adams, who was elected. The American people came to see Clay's support of Adams as corrupt. They suspected that he supported Adams for the presidency only after being assured the position of secretary of state. Adams made other political errors in office. Still alive were those who remembered not only his own Federalist origins but the Federalist position of his father as well. Adams promoted federal aid to states for improvements, aid to manufacturers, and the creation of a national tariff. It was the "Tariff of Abominations," however, that caused the most bitter opposition to his administration. With high duties on raw wool, hemp, flax, fur, and liquor, the tariff was at first opposed by New Englanders, who feared that the cost of raw materials needed in their factories would greatly increase. The Senate made enough concessions to the New England states to ensure their support, but Adams' political future was doomed. Opposition coalesed around Andrew Jackson, who defeated Adams in his bid for a second term in office.

All remaining vestiges of Federalism were cast out of national politics, and America's leanings toward sectional politics was complete. New England Yankees were now distinct characters in the American political scene. The independent Yankees had toyed with the idea of secession when the federal government seemed determined to ignore their concerns. Always eager to expand their business dealings, they carried on illegal smuggling activities when the government policies threatened to cut off their markets. They eyed with suspicion the increasing democratization of American politics. And, most importantly, the shrewd New England businessmen guarded the interests of manufacturing, paving the way for the hundreds of factories that were to be established throughout the region during the coming years.

A NEW WORKPLACE AND THE AGE OF REFORM

President Andrew Jackson stood for the common man. Enjoying massive support from all sections and social classes, he believed that the common man had an innate knowledge of good and evil and that he could accomplish anything he set out to do. Despite opposition over tariffs, and South Carolina's subsequent threat to nullify the national tariff law, Jackson won re-election in 1832 by a huge margin. Among his legacies was the Democratic Party, based on a belief in economic opportunities unhampered by government restrictions, a suspicion of special interests and large corporations, and a dedication to states' rights.

In opposition to the Democrats, the newly created Whig Party focused on the issue of strong fiscal policies; however the Whigs were unable to rally around a strong candidate for the presidential election of 1836. Their disunity ensured that Democratic Martin Van Buren would succeed President Jackson. Organizing and strengthening themselves over the next four years, the Whigs propelled their candidate General William Henry Harrison into the presidency in the 1840 election. Harrison lived only a month after his inauguration and was succeeded by John Tyler of Virginia.

One of the issues plaguing Tyler's administration was the dispute between the United States and Great Britain over the boundary between Maine and New Brunswick. Matters had escalated to the point that during 1839 more than two hundred Acadians had wintered on land claimed by Maine where they cut an estimated $100,000 worth of timber. Maine's legislature raised a large force, lumbermen and farmers later supplemented by thousands of militiamen, to patrol the disputed territory. In support of Maine, Congress called General Winfield Scott to the area and instructed him to negotiate a settlement favorable to the United States. Although fighting seemed almost inevitable, no bloodshed occurred: instead both sides agreed to a temporary plan to occupy the Aroostook Valley.

Daniel Webster, secretary of state under Tyler and a native of Salisbury, New Hampshire, was determined to settle the border dispute. In 1842, he and Lord Ashburton negotiated a treaty that bears

their names. Through the treaty, the British took possession of 5,000 square miles in northern Maine, while the United States maintained control of the area around a fort located at the northern end of Lake Champlain.

The image of the common man symbolized so eloquently by Jackson from 1828 to 1836 had changed dramatically from Jefferson's idealized view of yeoman farmers spread throughout the country where they worked small plots of their own land. To be sure, agriculture still predominated, but a new type of common man – the factory worker – had now entered the scene as well. During the 1820s the Industrial Revolution came full force to the northeast, and American workers began their long history of factory employment.

The factory system itself had roots in America dating back to the 1790 textile mill of Moses Brown and Samuel Slater. A former apprentice in Belper, England, Slater came to America armed with broad knowledge of the equipment on which he had worked in English textile mills. His memory of the equipment was extremely important to the infant textile industry, because England had not shared her industrial secrets, and Parliament had prohibited skilled workers from leaving the country. In order to leave England, Slater was forced to disguise himself as a farmer. He made his way to America where he soon sought out Moses Brown, owner of a spinning mill in Rhode Island. Brown financed the improvements designed by Slater – carding machines, water frames, and other pieces of equipment. By December 1790, the new machinery was in operation at the firm of William Almy and Smith Brown.

Brown had been dabbling in mechanization for a few years before Slater's arrival in Rhode Island. He had tried to install manually operated spinning and carding machines in his spinning factory in Providence. He then added water power to his cotton mill in Pawtucket, but the machinery was inefficient. Nowhere could he find mechanics who could build and operate the new machinery. Slater's arrival in Rhode Island was a turning point in Brown's industry. In addition to spinning yarn,

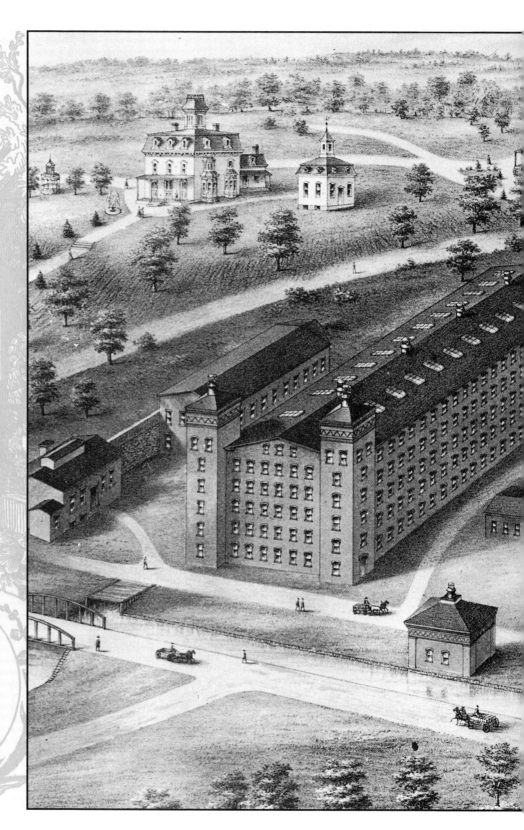

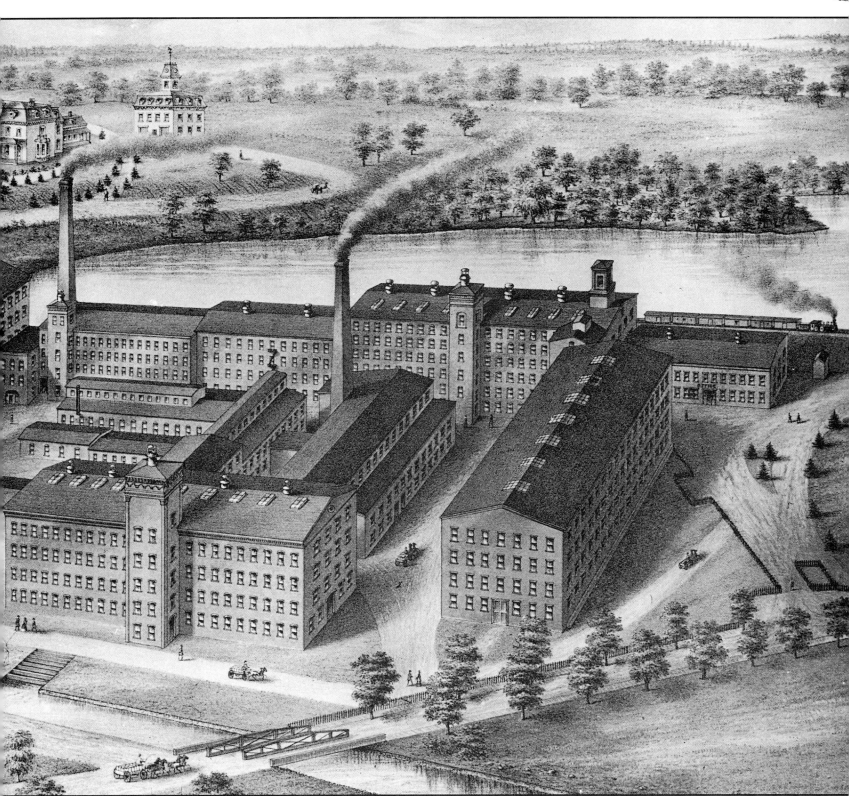

workers at the factory that Slater and Brown created also wove cloth. Previously this chore had been farmed out to independent weavers working in their own homes. In the two-story mill building, employees worked sixty to seventy hours a week under conditions that led, in 1800, to the first workers' strike in America.

In 1815 William Gilmore built a power loom, the first in Rhode Island, but a decade and a half would pass before such looms were widespread. Among the advantages of their use was the fact that women and children could operate them. What once required hundreds of craftsmen could now be done by a smaller and cheaper labor force.

Water-powered industry was not a boon to everyone. Farmers had to contend with floods caused by the building of mill dams; fishermen had to contend with diminished catches in streams and rivers leading to the dams. And everyone suffered when textile mills dumped wastes, bleach, and dyes into the rivers and streams.

Throughout New England, a shift in the economy occurred before and during the War of 1812. Heavily reliant on shipping and trading, the New England merchants were severely hurt by Jefferson's Embargo Act and by Britain's and France's commercial warfare. During the war itself, the merchants enjoyed a little more prosperity, due in no small part to their smuggling activities, but when England returned to her dominant position in trade after the war, New England shipowners and traders faced fierce competition. Of all the trading centers in Massachusetts, only Boston regained prominence in the overseas trade.

In the inland areas of Massachusetts, people had manufactured items for sale or trade since the Revolution. Farming there had been on the decline since the mid-eighteenth century, as there was simply not enough land to support the growing population. Steady streams of settlers moved from crowded Massachusetts and Connecticut to Vermont, New Hampshire, and Maine, and later into New York and Ohio. Those who remained turned to the operation of gristmills, sawmills, paper mills, and carding and fulling mills. They also

During the 1840s, Irish immigrants poured into America's sea coast towns, and by the end of the decade, New England's homogeneous population was no more. Previous pages: a typical Irish Emigrant Office, this one located on Ann Street in New York in 1845.

Living conditions for the newly arrived Irish were often little better in America than they had been in Ireland. Boston in particular was overcrowded. Left: an unhappy immigrant contemplates returning home, in a lithograph by J.H. Bufford.

transformed their cottage industries, undertaken initially during the winter months, into full-time operations. Spinners, weavers, shoemakers, wagon builders, coopers, potters, and others created surpluses they could sell at market.

Tiny textile mills sprang up throughout Massachusetts after Slater's success in Rhode Island. Employing no more than about a hundred people, these mills presaged the more heavily capitalized efforts of Francis Cabot Lowell of Newburyport. Lowell had learned about the textile business during a two-year vacation in England. He devised a plan for a factory that would handle all the steps in cloth production – from raw materials to finished cloth. Calling on his merchant friends and forming the Boston Manufacturing Company, he raised the necessary capital to build his dream.

Lowell and his investor-friend Patrick Tracey Jackson selected the site of a paper mill on the Charles River in Waltham for their new factory's location. Throughout 1813 and 1814, the new company financed and supervised the construction of the factory. Although the English mills had once again flooded the American market with their cheaply produced goods after the War of 1812, forcing many small New England mills out of business, the Boston Manufacturing Company held its own with sales volumes increasing from $3,000 in 1815 to $345,000 in 1822.

Money was to be made in the textile business, and Patrick Tracey Jackson was determined to expand. He formed a new company, the Merrimack Manufacturing Company, and bought up land near the town of Chelmsford for the site of his mills. Investors not only financed the land acquisition: they also paid for the widening and deepening of the Merrimack Canal, for the erection of two mill buildings, and for installing equipment as well. By September 1823, the mills were in business. Three years later, the four square miles around the mills were separated from Chelmsford and formed into a new town named Lowell.

Such a large enterprise required more labor than the neighboring communities could supply. So the company brought workers over from the British Isles and built dormitories for the mill girls and row houses for families. By 1836, 18,000 people inhabited the town where there had been open fields less than two decades before. The new residents established schools and churches of several denominations – Catholic, Methodist, Baptist, Congregationalist, and Universalist. Mill girls in Lowell earned between $2.50 and $3.00 a week. Their board in the company-owned housing cost them $1.25 a week. Although they worked throughout the daylight hours, some months as long as twelve and a half hours a day, they still had some time for leisure activities. They took advantage of circulating libraries, published their own literary magazine called the *Lowell Offering*, organized sewing circles, and attended educational lectures.

American industry boomed, but it had to contend with a shortage of workers who could operate the newly installed machines. With more and more markets opening up, industrialists had to find a way to produce more goods at lower prices. One way they accomplished this was by lowering their standards. With a decline in quality came a decreased emphasis on attracting skilled workers who could claim higher wages. Children under the age of sixteen made up about 50 percent of the textile work force. The widespread use of child labor was unalarming to the population at large. In the early era of reliance on family farms for earnings, children had worked side-by-side with their parents in the fields, and New England families saw little difference in field work and factory work. Shoe-making in Massachusetts had already enjoyed a long tradition, ever since shoemakers and leather workers settled around the area of Lynn in the early seventeenth century. By 1860 more than 60,000 workers were making shoes in the state.

In a society that was becoming increasingly dependent on industry, mechanics were tremendously important. The new machines were initially made of wood and iron and required the skills of carpenters and blacksmiths, but by the 1850s the equipment was made predominantly of metal. While large textile mills and other industries usually employed their own machinists, independent shops did develop, such as the Whitin Machine Works in Northbridge where a full range of equipment needed for cotton cloth production was made.

The largest industries in Massachusetts were leather and shoe making, textiles, machine building, and metalworking, but a host of other specialized industries grew up as well. Workers in Bristol and Worcester counties made cutlery and edged tools. Quarry workers in Quincy supplied their surrounding area with building stone. Pulp and paper mills, the descendents of lumber mills, spread throughout the region. Fishing and whaling remained important to residents in Gloucester, Marblehead, Plymouth, Cape Cod, and New

Bedford. And with America's growing prosperity, manufacturers of consumer goods, such as clothing, furniture, musical instruments, and books, found ready markets.

Between 1790 and 1815, Rhode Island led the nation in the production of yarn and textiles. After the mills at Lowell were established, Massachusetts took the lead, but Rhode Island still held a large share of the industry, producing twenty percent of the yarn and fifteen percent of the cotton cloth made in America. By 1860 more than thirty percent of the work force in the state was employed in the textile industry. Most of these workers were women and children.

During the early years of the textile industry, woolen mills were not nearly as widespread as cotton mills because adequate mechanization had not been developed for working wool. By 1832, however, there were twenty-two woolen mills operating in Rhode Island. But Rhode Islanders did not rely on the textile industry alone for their

Henry David Thoreau lived by Walden Pond for many years. The rustic setting provided the perfect opportunity for Thoreau to carry out his experiments in self-reliance and to develop his ideas about the divinity of nature. Today the spot where Thoreau's simple cabin stood is marked by stone pillars.

Ralph Waldo Emerson's home, the Old Manse in Concord, Massachusetts, was the site of meetings of the Transcendental Club. Behind the white pickett fence, Emerson, along with Bronson Alcott, Henry David Thoreau and Margaret Fuller, wrote and edited The Dial, *a transcendentalist magazine published from 1840 to 1844.*

livelihood. Growing up around the state were businesses engaged in making steam engines, metal tools, jewelry, and silverware. The banking and insurance businesses followed quickly on the scene.

In Connecticut, citizens were determined to maintain a status quo, to remain tied to farming the land no matter how inadequate it was to meet the needs of the growing population.

In Maine, by 1820, 8,000 people were employed in lumber mills, tanneries, gristmills, and textile mills. In addition to producing finished cloth, Mainers and Vermonters also produced the raw materials, and in the years from 1810 to 1830 they imported large numbers of Spanish sheep. Initially protected by tariffs, the sheep raisers lost interest in the enterprise when the Democrats ended the policy of protecting American industry and the English began once again supplying America with raw wool.

New Hampshire's industry at first centered on the sawmill and the gristmill, but by 1810 its citizens also worked in tanneries, linseed-oil mills,

distilleries, iron foundries, nail factories, and paper mills. Most products made in the state were consumed there, with two notable exceptions: the ships built in Portsmouth and Concord coaches manufactured by Abbott, Downing and Company.

Lewis Downing started his company to produce springless buggies in Portsmouth in 1816. Ten years later, he opened his business to Stephen Abbot, who became a partner in the enterprise. The design of the Concord coach was a study in innovation. The body rode on leather cushions rather than on springs. The interior of the coach was artistically decorated, sometimes with red plush and French windows, and the exterior often featured paintings of political leaders, landscapes, and mythological characters. A staple of western migration, less ornate versions of the Concord coach carried thousands of New Englanders to new territories to seek their fortunes.

New Hampshire benefitted from progress in textile mechanization when Charles Robbins, a former employee of Slater's, came to New Ipswich.

155

In December 1804, the fifty-spindle mill Robbins built started production. Another Slater employee, John Field, started a mill in Peterborough. In much the same way, the Amoskeag Manufacturing Company got its start in Derryfield, a few miles south of Concord on the Merrimack River. Built by Benjamin Prichard, the mill had easy access to Boston by way of a four-day ride down a canal built a few years earlier to connect Concord to the trading center. Equally important were the Amoskeag Falls, which dropped about eighty feet in one mile, an excellent source of water power. Over the years, the Amoskeag Manufacturing Company grew slowly with impetus from outside investors including Samuel Slater. The company bought more and more land and laid out a town with squares, schools, churches, parks, and cemeteries. By 1846, the population of the new city of Manchester had grown from 50 (in 1838) to 10,000, and the 3,200 employees of the company made 22.5 million yards of cloth a year.

With all the new products New Englanders were making, the problem of getting manufactured goods to markets, or to trading ports such as Boston where they could be shipped to their final destinations, became more and more pressing. Throughout the country, improving transportation was critical. The enterprising Americans responded by ushering in a new revolution, the transportation revolution, resulting in miles and miles of new roads, canals, and railroads.

The steam engine had been invented in the early eighteenth century by Thomas Newcomen in England. Nearly a century later, in 1804, Oliver Evans of Delaware introduced his reciprocating steam engine, and within a few years, steam boats and steam-driven locomotives darted through the American landscape. Railroads in New England connected Boston and Providence by 1832, then spread from Providence to Stonington, Connecticut, and on to New York City. Worcester, Hartford, and Bristol were all soon connected to Providence. In northern New England, the Rutland and Burlington Railroad and the Vermont Central linked Burlington to Boston, and other legs spread into New York.

Linking Vermonters to their extremely important market in Canada was the Grand Trunk Railroad between Montreal and Portland. New Hampshirites used the railroad between Nashua (south of Manchester) to ship products to Lowell, and a major road soon connected Exeter to Boston. Vermonters sent products to new markets in the Great Lakes region along the Erie Canal, built in 1825, while another canal linked Lake Champlain to the Hudson River, thus giving inland Vermont access to New York City and the Atlantic Ocean.

These expanding systems of railroads, canals, and turnpikes were ambitious projects, but perhaps most ambitious of all was the plan of John Alfred Poor to link Europe to the American interior through a system of ships and trains. The first portion of his scheme was to build a railroad to link Portland to Halifax and Montreal. Next he wanted to create a line of ships between Halifax and Liverpool. Travelers from England would arrive in Halifax, and then travel south by rail to Bangor, Portland, and on to New York. Against him were posed the financiers of Boston who had already planned a railroad from that city, north through the Connecticut Valley to the Saint Lawrence. Poor somehow managed to persuade Canadian investors that the route between Portland and Montreal would be more favorable to Canadian trade than the route between Boston and Montreal. He got his charter for the Atlantic and St. Lawrence Railway from the Maine legislature, and the Canadians committed to financing the portion of the run in their country. By the time the line was complete, however, the railroad company was deeply in debt and was forced to lease the line to the Grand Trunk Railway Company of Canada.

Poor then turned his attention to his dream of connecting Bangor and Portland to an Atlantic ferry system. Armed with a new charter for the European and North American line, he set out to raise the necessary funds, but not until the middle of the Civil War was he ready to begin building. The first leg of the line, between Bangor and Saint John, was completed in 1871, but because of the poor quality of the construction, Poor was fired from the

Ralph Waldo Emerson (1803-1882) was a teacher of individualism. His writings, lectures, essays and poems are infused with a spirit of self-reliance. Around him a group of writers formed the Transcendental Club, but Emerson never fully retreated into transcendentalism. He was an active campaigner for abolition and other social reforms. Photograph from the collections of Harvard University.

Henry David Thoreau (1817-1862) began his career as a teacher and pencil-maker, but before long he retired to Walden Pond and devoted himself to living a completely self-reliant life. His theories on civil disobedience and passive resistance and his belief in the individual nature of man are explored in Walden.

company.

His fascination with railroads did not end with his dismissal from the European and North American Railroad Company. Instead, he began a new scheme – to build a railroad from Portland to Chicago and on to the west coast. In this plan, Portland would become the gateway to the West and on to Asia for Europeans, and Maine coastal towns would thrive with the new influx of travelers. He managed to get yet another charter from the Maine legislature for the Portland, Rutland, Oswego and Chicago Railroad Company, and to drum up support from the boards of trade in Chicago and Buffalo, but he was unable to persuade Portland investors to finance the line. Although Poor was the person chiefly responsible for bringing railroads to Maine, his vision was never that simple, and he died a disappointed man in September 1871.

Railroads, canals, and turnpikes were primarily responsible for speeding the growth of industry, but a rapid increase in the labor supply due to vast numbers of new immigrants also helped American industry gain worldwide prominence. European immigrants were attracted to America by the promise of jobs. Along with this pull factor, there also existed a push. Poor agricultural conditions in Europe, especially in Ireland where farmers suffered a potato blight and in Germany where they faced a series of crop failures, propelled tens of thousands of immigrants to America. While many of the German and Scandinavian immigrants moved west to farm, most of the Irish immigrants stayed close to where they landed in the eastern seaport towns.

While the tide of immigration strengthened industry, American society was hard hit by sharpened class divisions. Poor Irish immigrants were willing to work for any wage offered them, and native-born workers blamed them for driving the level of wages down. Blacks in the northeast were angry that the Irish took jobs that had traditionally been theirs. In the New England textile mills, young farm girls no longer held the majority of jobs available by 1860. The employers at the mills found that the Irish required fewer amenities than the young girls, and that they were more likely

to remain working at the mills for a long time, in contrast to the farm girls who often left the mills after a year or two.

Most factory workers earned less than $5 a week, well below the $10.37 that *New York Tribune's* Horace Greeley allocated so carefully in his widely publicized weekly budget for a family of five, and the low wages and huge numbers of new immigrants soon combined to create a new urban problem. Slums developed in all the major cities, and attendant to the urban problems came two very different new types of movements – nativist and reform.

From 1846 to 1856, a thousand Irish immigrants poured into Boston each month. Such a flood, for which the city was not prepared, generated class strife and anti-Catholic sentiments. A splinter of the Whig Party, called the "American" or "Know-Nothing Party," was in position to accommodate individuals who feared the huge tide of immigration. Originally a secret club whose members used the password, "I don't know," the party rallied behind the cause of limiting immigration, especially by Catholics. In Massachusetts, in the 1854 elections, the party won all the seats in the Senate, all but three seats in the House, and the governorship.

In Rhode Island, anti-Catholic sentiments were aroused during the "Dorr War" of 1840 to 1842. The conflict began when Thomas Dorr and his followers challenged the voting restrictions imposed on citizens by the state's constitution. A Harvard-trained lawyer and legislator (from 1834 to 1837), Dorr worked tirelessly not only on the suffrage issue but also on educational reform and abolition. By this time, Rhode Island was the only state that had retained property requirements for voting. In addition, the state had clung to its practice of allowing first-born sons of freemen to vote upon reaching adulthood, even though they themselves might own no property. With the increasing numbers of immigrants, and the transition from farm to city life, only one-third of adult males met the voting requirements. Anti-Catholic sentiments came to bear among the suffrage reformers when they grappled with the question of whether to extend voting rights to all adult males or only to native-born, white, adult males.

In every town throughout the state, chapters of the Rhode Island Suffrage Association generated support for a constitutional convention. The legislature called just such a convention but specified that only property-holders could elect delegates and that only this small minority would ratify any new constitution drafted. In response, the Suffrage Association invited all adult white males to elect delegates to the "People's Convention." Now two constitutions were drafted and put to a vote. Neither document included provisions for black suffrage. Both included property requirements for citizens who wished to vote on the matters of taxes and government spending, though the "People's Constitution" was less stringent.

In an extralegal election in December 1841, 13,944 adult white men voted for the People's Constitution; 52 voted against it. Dorr claimed a clear majority, but the legislature refused to recognize the document or the convention that drafted it. When the Constitutional Convention's document, called the "Landholders' Constitution," was put to a vote, Dorrites rallied the opposition. The document was defeated 8,689 to 8,013. Dorr and his followers may have expected the legislature to accept the People's Constitution since the Landholders' document had been voted down, but the legislature persisted in refusing to recognize the People's Constitution and continued governing the state under the old charter. The legislature also passed laws aimed directly at the activities of the Dorrites. The new laws forbade any overt action against the charter on penalty of charges of treason.

Supporters of the government claimed in speeches, newspaper articles, and broadsides that the People's Party was permeated with Irish Catholics, labor organizers, and other "riff-raff." Nothing would deter the Dorrites, however. They held elections in April 1842 in which Dorr was chosen governor. The Landholders also held elections, with Samuel Ward King being named governor.

After attempting without success to generate support for his cause from President Tyler, Governor Dorr made yet another move that was considered treasonous by Governor King's government. With a band of 243 armed men, Dorr marched on the Providence arsenal. Only the malfunction of cannons fired by his troops kept blood from being shed on the night of May 17, 1842. The next morning, his troops retreated. In June, he was ready again to overthrow the charter government by force. Gathering his band of supporters in Chepachet, near the Connecticut border, Dorr planned to march on Providence. The charter government's army of 2,500 troops, among them many black residents of Providence, advanced toward Chepachet. Hopelessly outnumbered, the Dorr army disbanded, and their leader escaped to New Hampshire.

The charter government called for another constitutional convention and put the resulting document to a vote. Ratified in 1843, the new constitution gave voting rights to both black and white adult males. Although this constitution denied state and federal voting rights to naturalized citizens without property, it was a clear departure from the old days when Rhode Island's officials were elected by only a third of the adult male populace. In fact, the total size of the electorate increased 60 percent.

Anti-Catholicism, which had raised its head as a side issue in the Dorr War, became more prevalent in the late 1840s. The Order of the Star-Spangled Banner and other nativist societies were founded throughout New England as Irish immigrants flocked to urban areas. In Rhode Island, the Know-Nothing Party, reaching its peak in membership in the early 1850s, proposed a slate of candidates for the 1856 election. Their success was due in no small part to the furor growing out of a rumor that the Sisters of Mercy in Providence were holding a young woman against her will. Guarding the convent gates, the bishop and his small group of supporters narrowly avoided an attack by an angry mob.

Connecticut's politics were dominated by the Know Nothings during this time. Governor T. Minor

The poet and critic William Cullen Bryant (1794-1878) was an advocate of social reform. He was born in Cummington, Massachusetts, and for a time he practiced law in Great Barrington. Later he entered the world of publishing in New York City, where he bought the New York Evening Post on which he worked as an editor. Photograph by Brady.

B-2764

Nathaniel Hawthorne (1804-1864), from Salem, Massachusetts, immersed himself in the examination of good and evil. His book, The Scarlet Letter, *about a Puritan woman who was labeled as an adulterer, marks the birth of the symbolic novel in America. Photograph by Brady.*

proposed legislation that would lengthen the period of residence required before immigrants could be naturalized. He also proposed the dissolution of militia units whose members were foreign-born.

Leaders of the Know-Nothing Party played on Yankee fears that the newly arrived Irish immigrants would soon seize political power. But as politicians began to realized that the tide of immigration was necessary to support industry, attitudes became more moderate. At the end of the Civil War, during which many immigrants had fought for the Union, nativist political stances were all but gone. But during the 1850s, the problems of immigrants were seen to be of their own making. Most people viewed the immigrants' customs and religion as alien, and the squalid conditions in which they lived as deserved. An enlightened few soon came to the defense of immigrants, and other factory workers and urban dwellers, proposing all sorts of social reforms.

The formation of Working Men's societies were early attempts by laborers to improve their conditions – not only on the job but within society at large. Established in the 1830s, the groups expressed a new awareness of their rights as men. What members of these early labor organizations wanted was plain. In fact, their demands were spelled out weekly in the *Working-Man's Gazette*, published in Woodstock, Vermont: "Equal Universal Education. Abolition of Imprisonment for Debt. Abolition of all Licensed Monopolies. An entire Revision, or Abolition of the present Militia System. A Less Expensive Law System. Equal Taxation on Property. An Effective Lien Law for Laborers. All Officers to be Elected by the People. No Legislation on Religion" (quoted in *Social Ferment in Vermont, 1791-1850)*.

Little change occurred until later in the century, when workers organized labor unions that carried sufficient weight to demand improvements. Many states did pass legislation decreasing to eleven hours a day the length of time a factory could force its employees to work, and laws were also passed to protect children. In Rhode Island, for example, Welcome Sayles' extensive study of child labor

resulted in legislation that prohibited employers from hiring children under the age of twelve and forced them to provide time off for three months of school each year.

Another early reform that New Englanders pursued involved one of their primary sources of wealth. Rum had made many rich, but by 1855, laws were passed in twelve states and one territory prohibiting, or at least limiting, the use of alcoholic beverages. At first the temperance movements concentrated on the population itself. Leaders persuaded individuals to sign pledges that they would drink no more. They pressurized local merchants and hotels to remove liquor from their shelves. Farmers, who nearly always operated distilleries on their farms, shut them down – either because of their adoption of the temperance principles or because demand for their product had decreased.

Temperance leaders then aimed their attention at the use of liquor at public gatherings. Soon, rum was no longer served at funerals, marriages, militia trainings, house raisings, or clergy ordinations. Little time would pass before the movement leaders were ready to tackle state laws. They often began their activity in the state arena by persuading legislators to withhold liquor licenses. Next, they sent petitions to their legislatures urging the passage of prohibition laws. Sometimes temperance leaders themselves were instrumental in writing such laws, as was the case in Maine with Neal Dow.

Dow was convinced that Maine's lack of prosperity and growth was due to the consumption of liquor – a practice he believed was widespread among its citizens. He brought his fight to the state level when his friend, Edward Kent, was elected governor in 1838. From his position on the governor's staff, Dow pushed the cause of the Maine Temperance Union for total abstinence. First, he persuaded hundreds of people in Portland to sign pledges of abstinence. Next, he pushed Portland's city leaders to hold a public referendum on prohibition. Then he was ready to take on the state. Presenting to the legislature a petition bearing 3,800 signatures, Dow succeeded in swaying the

legislators to his cause, and his famous "Maine Law" was passed in 1851. The law prohibited the manufacture of liquor and incorporated severe penalties for infractions.

The American Society for the Promotion of Temperance, founded in 1826 in Boston, had state and local chapters spring up throughout New England. In 1840, a different kind of organization was formed in Boston – the Washington Movement, which sought to reform individuals addicted to alcohol. Converts reached by this group were called what they were, "Reformed Drunkards." During their meetings, former drinkers would share their experiences, both the degradations of their life of drink and the joys of their recovery. These new tactics drew huge crowds.

The temperance movement in New England brought about a complete shift in public opinion. Whereas drinking alcoholic beverages had been not merely condoned but encouraged, by mid-century it was viewed with disdain. From the movement grew organizations that can best be described as self-help or improvement societies, which quickly transformed themselves into humanitarian organizations led by a growing body of social workers. Through the temperance movement, these people gained experience and knowledge that they put to use in other reforms, such as welfare movements and abolition.

One of the demands of the Working Men's societies – the abolition of imprisonment for debt – spurred reforms of the penal system as a whole. Many states had built penitentiaries early in the nineteenth century, but little had been done over the years to maintain or enlarge them. Overcrowding was chronic, and many of the enlightened citizens of the day were dismayed at the exploitation of prisoners in income-producing activities. The Prison Discipline Society, founded in 1825, led to reforms. The society's leader, the Reverend Louis Dwight, expanded the group's early mission of prison reform to encompass wider issues, including the care of the insane, the separation of juvenile offenders from adult criminals, and the education of the deaf and dumb.

Reform of the penal system brought about some interesting experiments. One of the new theories put into practice during this time was the "silent system," in which inmates worked together in shops in total silence during the day and returned to their individual cells at night.

Dorothea Dix was extremely active in prison reform and in the care of the insane. Born in Hampden, Maine, in 1802, Dix moved to Massachusetts at the age of twelve, first to live with her grandmother and then with her great-aunt. Her involvement with prison reform began in 1841 when she taught Sunday school class to women inmates of the East Cambridge jail. Among the prisoners, she found many mentally ill women who were treated cruelly even though they had committed no crime. Taking their case to the Middlesex Court, she effected a renovation of the jail with better facilities for the mentally ill. She then undertook a tour of all penal facilities in the state – county jails, almshouses, and state facilities. After reviewing Dix's findings, the general court approved funds for expanding Worcester State Hospital – a mental illness facility that had been founded in 1833 through the work of Horace Mann. Dix's influence soon spread beyond Massachusetts. Touring many states, and then moving on to the European continent, she became the best-known American woman of her day.

Horace Mann not only worked on reforms for the care of the mentally ill, but also brought about drastic changes in the educational system. As a result of his efforts, students went to school for more months each year, teachers received higher wages, and schools were established to train teachers.

Extremist reform movements also flourished during the years before the Civil War. John Humphrey Noyes, for example, established a communal society at Putney, Vermont. Perfectionism combined religious, social, and economic theories to create an ideal society. Noyes and his followers met with resistance from the local community, however, when they began sharing wives and formed a committee to pair couples for

Previous pages: the House of Seven Gables, Captain John Turner's house, at 54 Turner Street in Salem, Massachusetts. Nathaniel Hawthorne wrote his masterpiece, The House of Seven Gables, *while living in Lenox. Its story of decadence brought Hawthorne increased attention and fame. While it is unlikely that Hawthorne used the house in Salem as the precise setting for his book, he no doubt modeled the setting after the house, which he had visited as a child.*

Nathaniel Hawthorne and his bride Sophia Peabody lived for four years at Ralph Waldo Emerson's home, the Old Manse (left), in Concord, Massachusetts. While living there, Hawthorne wrote Mosses from an Old Manse, *first published serially and then as a single volume.*

The poet Henry Wadsworth Longfellow (1807-1882), from Portland, Maine, produced a huge body of work during his lifetime. While living in Craigie House (overleaf) – now known as Longfellow House – in Cambridge, Massachusetts, Longfellow taught at Harvard for many years. Upon retiring from the College, he continued his writings, publishing The Song of Hiawatha *in 1855 and* The Courtship of Miles Standish *in 1858. These and other poems, such as* The Wreck of the Hesperus *and* The Village Blacksmith, *were widely acclaimed during his day and remain standards of romantic literature.*

Herman Melville (1819-1891) lived at Arrowhead near Pittsfield, Massachusetts, from 1850 to 1863. His masterpiece, Moby-Dick: or the White Whale *centers around the whaling industry in New England while it explores man's preoccupation with evil, a preoccupation that over time causes evil to invade the character of man. Photograph by Rockwood.*

the purpose of breeding children. By 1847, the Putney Community moved to Oneida, New York, where they continued their "complex" marriages in the face of resistance from the orthodox clergy.

Shakers, or the United Society of Believers in Christ's Second Coming, began in New Lebanon, New York. In New Hampshire, communities of Shakers settled in Canterbury and Enfield. Believing in celibacy, communal property, and self-sacrificing hard work, the Shakers in Canterbury became well known and prosperous through the sale of flatbrooms and washing machines. Enfield's Shakers packaged seed and produced the Eclipse Corn Planter for sale.

The Age of Jackson saw the beginning of the New England Renaissance. The age was a time of great social change as evidenced not only by the large number of reform movements but also by the body of literature – both reform and romantic – produced during this time. In New England, a group of writers proposed a new order and described the changes that were taking place and those that were to come. Nathaniel Hawthorne, William Cullen Bryant, George Bancroft, Washington Irving, and others supported the Democratic Party and the common man it represented. These individuals did more than just examine the American scene and suggest reforms: they actively participated in political life to effect the changes they proposed.

In contrast to these Democratic writers were the transcendentalists, who did not hold much faith in Jackson and the Democratic Party. While both groups of writers espoused striving for perfection and self-reliance, the transcendentalists followed a much more individualistic path. They withdrew not only from politics, but from society as well, preferring instead to contemplate truth in isolation. As inspiration for their movement, they took the writings of the German writer Immanuel Kant who described the intuitive knowledge of man. Transcendentalists went a step further: they elevated intuition over reason and devised a doctrine that had at its core a belief in the "Oversoul" present in all things.

Some of the transcendentalists experimented with communal living at Brook Farm. The brainchild of educational reformer and former Unitarian preacher George Ripley, the farm was home to more than 140 people during its prime. By day, residents worked the farm, attended lectures on German philosophers, or taught or attended the farm school. At night, these free spirits engaged in activities that residents of other communal societies would never have condoned: they held dancing parties and Shakespeare readings, they produced plays and pageants, or they walked to nearby Boston to attend concerts or lectures.

A new breed of writers was on the scene. America was coming of age, and these new writers capitalized on a rich heritage never before explored in literature. The New England Renaissance began as an intellectual movement eloquently explored by Emerson and Thoreau and later by Hawthorne, Longfellow, Holmes, and Lowell. This new literature centered on Democratic idealism expressed through a romantic vision. The Romantics rebelled against the formalism of the neoclassical period and against the Age of Reason. Feeling was more important to the romantic than logic. In addition, these writers capitalized on the lyceum movement that had begun in the 1830s. At public addresses, crowds thronged to hear speeches and to enjoy debate with their neighbors.

The philosophies of Ralph Waldo Emerson fell somewhere between those of the Democratic writers and the pure transcendentalists. At first an active member of the Whig Party, Emerson withdrew from it when Daniel Webster came out in support of the Compromise of 1850, which included the Fugitive Slave Bill so hated in New England. He abandoned as well his early calling as a minister in the Unitarian Church, turning instead to preaching about the divinity and inherent self-reliance of each individual. His brand of individualism was widely accepted among members of his audience who were energized by the dynamic creativity Emerson explored in them. Many of his lectures were later published in *Nature* (1836), *Essays* (1841), and *Essays: Second Series* (1844). His poems, however,

hold the germ of his philosophy, and they too were published in *Poems* (1847), *May-Day and Other Poems* (1867), and other works. Perhaps the most quoted line from Emerson's poetry comes from "Concord Hymn," in which he eulogized the lowly farmers who defended America in the Revolutionary War:

By the rude bridge that arched the flood
Their flag to April's breeze unfurled,
Here once the embattled farmers stood
And fired the shot heard round the world.

Around Emerson, a circle of writers formed the Transcendental Club, which met at Emerson's house, the Old Manse, in Concord. Among the club's members were Bronson Alcott, Henry David Thoreau, and Margaret Fuller, who served as the first editor of *The Dial*, the club's magazine. Emerson could never bring himself to accept the isolation of Brooks Farm or Thoreau's Walden Pond. Instead, he remained in the world, commenting on it and after 1850 becoming more and more involved in abolition and other social reforms.

Henry David Thoreau began work on his *Journals*, his largest work of all, while a student at Harvard College. For a time, Thoreau taught school in Concord, helped his father in his pencil-making business, and traveled on a lecture circuit. He hated what he saw around him – men working in factories reduced to small parts of a whole. While he in no way advocated the abandonment of city or factory life for others, he himself found no home in society. He withdrew to Walden Pond, where he lived in a tiny hut year-round, tending to his needs for food and shelter and writing his *Journals*. His book, entitled *Walden*, explains his reasons for withdrawing from society: "I went to the wood because I wished to live deliberately, to front only the essential facts of life, and see if I could not learn what it had to teach, and not, when I came to die, discover that I had not lived."

Thoreau's activism was in response to issues that affected him personally. He refused to pay church

Longfellow's epic poem Evangeline *brought the writer great fame. G.R. Grant, his artistic imagination inspired by this poem, portrayed the home of Evangeline in an engraving (previous pages).*

Left: a photograph of Oliver Wendell Holmes (1809-1894) by Lowell M. Max. Holmes lived in Cambridge, Massachusetts, where he was not only a successful writer but also a doctor, and Professor of Medical Science at Harvard. He wrote the impassioned poem Old Ironsides *after learning that the historic frigate USS* Constitution, *active in the War of 1812, was to be demolished in Charlestown Navy Yard. The poem, printed in Boston's* Daily Advertiser *on September 16, 1830, generated such a public outcry that the old ship was saved from demolition.*

taxes to the state because they were earmarked for what he saw as an "established" church. He refused to pay the Massachusetts poll tax, because of Massachusetts' support of the Mexican War and the system of slavery. His essay "Civil Disobedience" contains the philosophy behind these actions and the core of the concept of passive resistance. His book *Walden*, however, was the heart of his work, exploring the divinity of nature, championing man and individualism, and attacking the materialistic character he saw pervading American life.

The common man was the central character in Romantic literature. Nathaniel Hawthorne and Herman Melville turned a celebration of the common man, seen in Emerson's and Thoreau's works, into a psychological and moral exploration. The writings of Longfellow, Lowell, and Holmes are filled with the spirit of reform. John Greenleaf Whittier became so engaged in the abolition movement that he had little time left for his writing.

William Cullen Bryant dealt with humanitarian reform and morality as well as with religion and nature in his poetry and criticism. Born in Cummington, in western Massachusetts, Bryant practiced law for a time in Great Barrington. With the publication of "Thanatopsis" in 1817, in which he attacked the rigid Calvinism of the day, he became widely known as an American writer. Espousing the liberal Democratic Party policies, he wrote and spoke in favor of freedom of speech, religion, and labor association.

With Nathaniel Hawthorne, the school of American symbolism arrived. Born in Salem, he lived for a time in Maine and then at Brook Farm and Emerson's home in Concord. Immersed in the study of evil and morality, Hawthorne became widely known with the publication, in 1850, of *The Scarlet Letter*, the first American symbolic novel. After the Democrats lost control of the government, and Hawthorne lost his position as a surveyor in the Custom House in Salem, Concord became his permanent home. There he wrote his other masterpiece, *The House of Seven Gables*.

Just a year after the publication of *The Scarlet Letter,* another Romantic writer brought out his

symbolic novel *Moby Dick.* A native of New York, Herman Melville settled at Arrowhead, near Pittsfield, Massachusetts, where he completed the novel that explores one of the great occupations of New England – whaling. Through the adventure tale, he infused the character of Captain Ahab with an intense preoccupation with evil, embodied in the whale Moby Dick, and later, in *Billy Budd, Sailor*, he reconciled himself to the fact that innocents suffer at the hand of evil that is inherent in nature.

The poet Henry Wadsworth Longfellow was widely read in his day. Born in Portland, Maine, he attended and later became a professor at Bowdoin College. Accepting a professorship at Harvard, he produced a remarkable body of work from 1839 to 1849. Popular among his countrymen for works such as *The Wreck of the Hesperus* and *The Village Blacksmith* (published in *Ballads and Other Poems*), for *The Arsenal at Springfield* (published in *The Belfry of Bruges and Other Poems*), and for *Evangeline*, an epic of great vividness, he also

A photograph of James Russell Lowell (1819-1891) taken by Oliver Wendell Holmes. Lowell was a man of many parts. He worked for humanitarian causes, edited the Atlantic Monthly*, wrote such noted classics as* The Bigelow Papers*, taught modern languages at Harvard and served as the U.S. ambassador to Spain and Great Britain. The* Bigelow Papers *were popular for their outspoken opposition to the Mexican War.*

Emily Dickinson (1830-1886), from Amherst, Massachusetts, wrote in a simple style distinguished by its passion. Only seven of her hundreds of poems were published during her lifetime. Today her home is owned by Amherst College.

turned his attention to stories of Indians and the Plymouth Colony with the publication of *The Song of Hiawatha* and *The Courtship of Miles Standish*, and with them gained even greater recognition both in America and abroad.

The work of John Greenleaf Whittier was first seen by Americans in the pages of William Lloyd Garrison's *Liberator*, the most widely read journal of abolitionism. A native of Haverhill, Massachusetts, the Quaker poet spent much of his time working for abolition, serving as a delegate to the National Anti-Slavery Convention in Philadelphia in 1833 and as a member of the Massachusetts legislature for one term. In 1836, Whittier settled in Amesbury, Massachusetts, where he continued to write in support of abolition. Known throughout much of his life as a reformer, he received wide attention for his literary works with the publication of *Snow Bound* in 1866.

Oliver Wendell Holmes, born of a well-to-do family in Cambridge, Massachusetts, was a natural writer who spent much of his time in a different occupation – as a doctor and professor of medical science. Dean of the Harvard Medical School from 1847 to 1853, he devoted his spare time to literature. Readers of his day revelled in the humor of his verse and his allegorical works, such as "The Deacon's Masterpiece," in which he humorously lays open the fallacies of Puritan logic in Jonathan Edwards' *The Freedom of the Will*.

James Russell Lowell, of Cambridge, Massachusetts, was no less a humanitarian than a writer. Abolition and other social reforms fed his writings with zeal. After serving as the first editor of the *Atlantic Monthly,* he and his wife Maria White, a noted abolitionist, lived for a time in Philadelphia, where Lowell edited *The Pennsylvania Freeman.* Returning to Cambridge and his ancestral home of Elmwood, he received wide attention for *The Biglow Papers,* which appeared serially in the Boston *Courier.* Through this series, he attacked the United States' policy toward Mexico and the Mexican War using the voice of Hosea Biglow – a voice filled with Yankee dialect and humor. During the Civil War, he again brought out the voice of

Hosea in satires on the Confederacy and defenses of Northern policies. His poetry began circulating with the publication of *A Year Life* (1841), *Poems* (1844), *Poems: Second Series* (1848), and *The Vision of Sir Launfal* (1848). As joint editor of the *North American Review,* as the Smith Professor of Modern Languages at Harvard, and as ambassador to Spain and Great Britain, Lowell embraced the world around him.

These writers – Emerson, Thoreau, Hawthorne, Melville, Whittier, and the rest – were founders of a new American tradition in literature, a tradition that used American stories and legends, American places, and American experiences to forge new symbols. Their work, and the writings of New Englanders Emily Dickinson later in the nineteenth century and Robert Frost in the twentieth century, brought Americans to the brink of abandoning their almost total reliance on England for things cultural. These New Englanders have found an important place in history not only because of their classic works but also because of their activism, their work for reform.

Improved education, prison reform, adequate care for the mentally ill – these were causes that New Englanders could rally round with conviction in the mid-nineteenth century. The movements grew from a new wave of revivalism that stressed the ability of all good Christians to attain salvation. They grew from the work of the transcendentalists, such as Emerson and Thoreau, who wrote that man could achieve perfection through striving for reform. They grew as well from Americans' firm belief in progress. But two reform movements flew in the face of strong beliefs. The issues of women's rights and the abolition of slavery caused bitter resentments among Americans. The first would not be resolved until 1920, with the passage of the Nineteenth Amendment; the second would precipitate a devastating Civil War.

TO BE SOLD & LET

BY PUBLIC AUCTION,

On MONDAY the 18th of MAY. 1829,

UNDER THE TREES.

FOR SALE,

THE THREE FOLLOWING

SLAVES,

VIZ.

HANNIBAL, about 30 Years old, an excellent House Servant, of Good Character.

WILLIAM, about 35 Years old, a Labourer.

NANCY, an excellent House Servant and Nurse.

The MEN belonging to "LEECH'S" Estate, and the WOMAN to Mrs. D. SMIT

TO BE LET,

On the usual conditions of the Hirer finding them in Food, Clothing, and Medical Attendance,

THE FOLLOWING

MALE and FEMALE

SLAVES,

OF GOOD CHARACTERS.

ROBERT BAGLEY, about 20 Years old, a good House Servant.

WILLIAM BAGLEY. about 18 Years old, a Labourer.

JOHN ARMS, about 18 Years old.

JACK ANTONIA. about 40 Years old, a Labourer.

PHILIP. an Excellent Fisherman.

HARRY. about 27 Years old, a good House Servant.

LUCY, a Young Woman of good Character, used to House Work and the Nursery.

ELIZA, an Excellent Washerwoman.

CLARA, an Excellent Washerwoman.

FANNY, about 14 Years old, House Servant.

SARAH. about 14 Years old, House Servant.

Also for Sale, at Eleven o'Clock,

Fine Rice, Gram, Paddy, Books, Muslins, Needles, Pins, Ribbons, &c. &c.

AT ONE O'CLOCK, THAT CELEBRATED ENGLISH HORSE

BLUCHER,

ABOLITION, CIVIL WAR, AND WOMEN'S RIGHTS

Facing page: a leaflet announces a slave auction on May 18, 1829. Although the only location given for the sale is "under the trees," the leaflet is most likely to originate from one of the Southern states or from the West Indies.

The issue of slavery was not divided neatly along geographical lines. Northern merchants and shipowners had grown wealthy on the profits of the triangular trade, and after the spread of cotton mills throughout New England, wealthy industrialists supported the Southern plantation owners in their efforts to maintain the institution of slavery. Slave labor was crucial to cotton growing, and the large mills of New England needed more and more cotton every year. Some historians have labeled the cooperation of Northern industrialists and Southern plantation owners a "conspiracy of silence."

In the eighteenth century, more slaves lived in Rhode Island than in any other New England state. Through the efforts of the Quakers, Baptists, and Congregationalists, the number steadily dwindled, falling from almost twelve percent of the total population in 1755 to about six percent in 1774. An early effort at emancipation came during the Revolutionary War, when the general assembly bought Rhode Island slaves to form the Black Regiment, and subsequently freed those who fought

Right: an engraving of a slave coffle.

CHAPTER FIVE

The peculiar "Domestic Institutions of our Southern brethren."

Selling a Mother from her Child.

Mothers with your Children at work in the field.

A Woman chained to a Girl, and a Man in irons at work in the field.

"They can't take care of themselves"; explained in an interesting article.

Hunting Slaves with dogs and guns. A Slave drowned by the dogs.

Servility of the Northern States in arresting and returning fugitive Slaves.

The front page of the September 2, 1839, issue of The Emancipator, *published in New York City, one of many anti-slavery tracts circulated in the North.*

In 1744 A Journal of the Proceedings in the Detection of the Conspiracy *(right) contained an account of a supposed plot by free blacks and slaves in New York City to burn the city and kill its inhabitants. In such ways tensions over slavery mounted slowly, began to dominate the political scene, and eventually contributed to the causes of a dreadful civil war. The anti-slavery message spread in William Lloyd Garrison's* The Liberator *did not always fall on welcoming ears. Garrison faced angry mobs wherever he went. Far right: three different banners from the newspaper, dating from 1831 to 1850. Its motto remained the same: "Our Country is the World – Our Countrymen are All Mankind."*

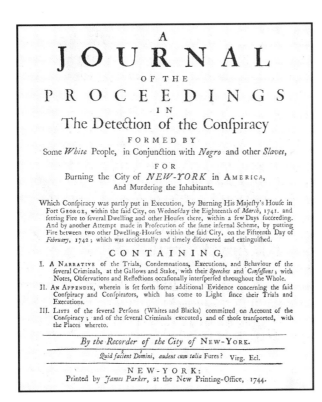

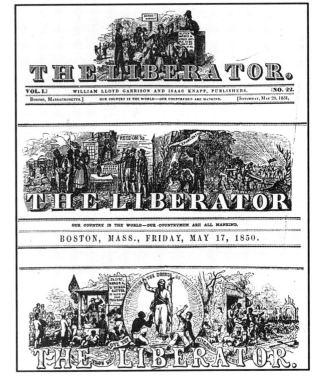

in the war. Slavery was gradually phased out by a law passed in 1784, calling for the emancipation of all children born to slave mothers after March 1, 1784. By 1859, no slaves lived in the state. However, the slave trade remained active in Rhode Island even after the gradual emancipation law went into effect. Slave traders devised methods of circumventing the 1787 law that called for the fining of owners of Rhode Island ships caught in the trade. The shipowners either bribed customs officials to look the other way or used Connecticut ports for their vessels until, in 1788, that state also passed a law restricting slave trade.

Samuel Hopkins, James Manning, and Moses Brown, whose brother John was an active slave trader, created the Providence Society for Abolishing the Slave Trade in 1789. This early antislavery group financed the prosecution of people engaged in the slave trade and started a night school for blacks. Blacks in Rhode Island established the African Union Society and the African Benevolent Society. Newport Gardner (or

Occramer Marycoo) led these organizations and coordinated their efforts with white abolitionists. In 1823, however, Gardner lost heart when a law was passed prohibiting blacks from voting, and he left Rhode Island and America for Africa.

The constitutions written by the Landholders and the People's Party during the Dorr War did not call for enfranchising blacks, but abolitionists rallied to the aid of local black leaders during meetings in 1841 and 1842. In the end, the constitution that was ratified in 1843 gave black men the right to vote, in part as a reward for protecting Providence during Dorr's march on the city.

Slavery had existed in Connecticut from early colonial days, although the number of slaves there was never great. Individuals who held slaves usually owned no more than three. A series of colonial laws strictly governed the conduct of blacks. They were required to have passes for travel; they could not purchase alcohol; they were subject to a 9:00 p.m. curfew; and they were not allowed to trade with whites. These laws, in many

CHAPTER FIVE

CAUTION!!

COLORED PEOPLE
OF BOSTON, ONE & ALL,

You are hereby respectfully CAUTIONED and advised, to avoid conversing with the

Watchmen and Police Officers of Boston,

For since the recent ORDER OF THE MAYOR & ALDERMEN, they are empowered to act as

KIDNAPPERS
AND

Slave Catchers,

And they have already been actually employed in KIDNAPPING, CATCHING, AND KEEPING SLAVES. Therefore, if you value your LIBERTY, and the *Welfare of the Fugitives* among you, *Shun* them in every possible manner, as so many *HOUNDS* on the track of the most unfortunate of your race.

Keep a Sharp Look Out for KIDNAPPERS, and have TOP EYE open.

T O BE SOLD on board the Ship *Bance-Island*, on tuesday the 6th of *May* next, at *Ashley-Ferry*, a choice cargo of about 250 fine healthy

NEGROES,

just arrived from the Windward & Rice Coast. —The utmost care has already been taken, and shall be continued, to keep them free from the least danger of being infected with the SMALL-POX, no boat having been on board, and all other communication with people from *Charles-Town* prevented.
Austin, Laurens, & Appleby.

N. B. Full one Half of the above Negroes have had the SMALL-POX in their own Country.

cases, applied to free blacks as well as to slaves. As in Rhode Island, many Connecticut blacks earned their freedom by serving in the army during the Revolutionary War. After the war, the state passed a manumission law that freed all blacks born after March 1, 1784, when they reached the age of twenty-five, and in 1788 and 1790 the legislature passed laws to end the slave trade.

In New Hampshire, slavery existed in the colonial period, and shipowners in Portsmouth took part in the triangular trade. By 1820, however, there were no slaves living in the state. Other areas of northern New England – Vermont and Maine – had almost no slaves and very few free blacks within their borders.

Northern industrialists turned their heads away from the slavery controversy until 1829, when a Boston shop owner named David Walker published his *Appeal*. A free-born black from North Carolina, Walker urged slaves to rebel against their owners. Within the next two years another voice was heard – that of William Lloyd Garrison of Newburyport, Massachusetts. Through his publication called the *Liberator*, Garrison demanded the immediate abolition of slavery. He flooded New England with copies of the *Liberator,* and with pamphlets as well, and he established a lecture circuit with well-known speakers traveling throughout the region. Facing angry mobs wherever he went, Garrison at one point was dragged from the *Liberator's* building through the streets of Boston, and stripped to his underwear.

Garrison's message found sympathizers in New Hampshire, where slavery had died out of its own accord by 1820, and in Connecticut, where a manumission law had been passed. A chapter of the New England Antislavery Society was formed in Concord in 1834, and Garrison was a frequent lecturer in New Hampshire. The abolition movement came to Maine at the moment of statehood. Having been embroiled in the issue of expanding slavery in the territories, a conflict that resulted in Missouri's entering the Union as a slave state and Maine's admission as a free state, the citizens of Maine had an early dislike of the

The Fugitive Slave Law gave slave owners the right to reclaim their slaves in non-slave-holding states. Law officials were bound to assist owners in their efforts or face steep fines, imprisonment, or claims of civil damages. Left: a broadside warns the black population of Boston to stay away from policemen who might detain them and to guard against kidnapping. The broadside was written by Theodore Parker, a man active in the Vigilance Committee of Boston.

An advertisement announces a slave sale at Ashley Ferry. The importation of slaves to the United States was outlawed in 1808, but many ships and their crews circumvented the law and as many as 250,000 slaves were imported after the law was passed.

The Fugitive Slave Law was hated throughout the North. Its enforcement spurred abolitionists to greater action. Anti-slavery societies sprang up throughout New England. *Overleaf:* an engraving depicting an anti-slavery convention at Exeter Hall in 1841. Conservative New Englanders, mostly manufacturers and traders who feared a loss of business, continued to support reconciliation with the South up until the eve of the Civil War.

practice. About a decade later, Garrison traveled through Maine spreading his message of immediate emancipation. There he confronted the Reverend Cyril Pearl of the American Colonization Society. This group advocated the return of blacks to Africa. Its efforts made little difference to the population of New England and, unfortunately for the abolition movement, the society diverted the attention of New Englanders from abolition to relocation. By 1834, however, Mainers turned to abolition and created the Maine Antislavery Society.

Garrison and members of the various abolition societies met with resistance and even violence during the 1830s. Even those who did not actively pursue abolition through membership in these organizations faced resistance whenever their actions countered society's standards. Prudence Crandall, for example, was driven from her home in Canterbury, Connecticut, for admitting to her school for young women Sarah Harris, the daughter of a prosperous black farmer. When the town's citizens withdrew their daughters from the school, Crandall decided to turn the institution into one devoted solely to the education of young black women. She and her students braved months of abuse. Even after the Connecticut legislature passed a law stipulating that a town must approve any school for out-of-state students, Crandall refused to close her doors. Instead, she was jailed until the Reverend Samuel J. May, a local abolitionist leader, posted her bail. Crandall continued to operate her school until September 1834, when a mob broke into the building and vandalized it. Unable to pay for repairs, Crandall and her new husband, Calvin Philleo, closed the school and moved to the Midwest.

Crandall was only one of many New England women who took up the cause of abolition. Female Antislavery Societies were created throughout the region, and many women opened their homes to escaped slaves traveling north along the "Underground Railroad." But because they were women, their presence at meetings of the American Antislavery Society and other male-dominated abolition organizations was not welcome. Indeed,

I consider Slavery as a Curse , a curse to the Master a grievous wrong to the Slave , in the abstract, it is all wrong, and no possible contingency can make it right. I am Mr. President no friend to slavery."

"Neither am I a friend to Duelling, not I!

Never mind, I hold a cool Sixty Slaves myself & "I will continue to oppose any scheme, whatever of emancipation, gradual or immediate".

Yet I take a shot whenever it suits me.

"I maintain that an oppressed people are authorized whenever they can, to rise & break their fetters." (1818.)

Mason & Dixon's Line.

Well done Hal, your o Liberty are gone . You in its true light a for free institutions shake of your dade made President for

*ty & delusion about
beginning to see Slavery
most safe & stable basis
world". Give us a
y worthy! you shall be*

when Garrison managed to force the New England Antislavery Society to allow women onto the convention floor, eight ministers resigned from the organization.

Lydia Maria Child made a strong mark on the cause of abolition. The author of such noted works as *The Frugal Housewife, The Mother's Book*, and *The Little Girl's Own Book*, Child turned her attention to slavery in *An Appeal in Favor of That Class of Americans Called Africans*. In the work she spoke out in favor of abolition as opposed to colonization, and although the publication was protested everywhere in 1833, it reached thousands of homes where women readers took up the cause. Child lost some of her devoted readers by taking a stand on the slavery issue, but she persisted in her abolition activities by writing more articles and editing the *National Anti-Slavery Standard*.

Maria Weston Chapman of Boston worked tirelessly to establish Female Antislavery Societies in Massachusetts. She also edited the *Liberator* whenever Garrison needed her help, and raised money for the cause through fairs and bazaars.

The efforts of women, such as Chapman and Child, brought to a head a conflict within the abolition movement itself – the question of whether women should be afforded an equal voice in the running of the movement. At a meeting of the American Antislavery Society in New York, Abby Kelley was elected to a position on the business committee. Three other women were elected to the executive committee. Crying that Garrison had packed the house with supporters of female equality, Arthur and Lewis Tappan and other leaders withdrew from the organization and formed the American and Foreign Antislavery Society. From the 1840s on, the two national groups competed with each other for members and quarrelled over tactics.

Relentless in his struggle to achieve the abolition of slavery was John Quincy Adams. Having lost his bid for re-election to the presidency in 1828, Adams returned home to Quincy, Massachusetts, but within two years he entered political life again as a congressman from his state. On the House floor,

Adams was determined to speak the unspeakable – to bring to the forefront a discussion of slavery. Every day, he read petitions for abolition from people throughout the country. When he faced a censure trial, even those New Englanders who were not abolitionists rallied to his side. In 1844, Adams led the fight to rescind the Gag Rule that had been in effect for eight years. The rule had stipulated that petitions for abolition sent to Congress would not be read aloud, but would be placed on a table for congressmen to read at their discretion. After the end of the Gag Rule, the way was open for discussion of slavery, but Adams never saw the resolution of the battle he fought for eighteen years. He collapsed in Congress on February 21, 1848, and died a few days later at the age of eighty one.

Frederick Douglass was the most well-known black abolitionist of the day. A former slave in Maryland, Douglass had escaped in 1838 and had settled in Massachusetts. In 1845, he published *Narrative of the Life of Frederick Douglass,* an account of his experiences as a slave. He proclaimed the need not only for the abolition of slavery but for full equality as well.

In New Hampshire, Nathaniel Peabody Rogers, editor of the *Herald of Freedom* in Concord, and Parker Pillsbury, editor of the *National Anti-Slavery Standard*, furthered the abolitionists' cause. The antislavery contingent and the proslavery contingent in the state had frequent clashes which often turned to violence. The poet John Greenleaf Whittier, for example, was attacked by an angry mob throwing eggs when he spoke in Concord.

Abolition and the expansion of slavery into new states and territories was *the* political issue of the 1840s and 1850s, and the political parties were rife with debate that culminated in the formation of new parties. The Liberty Party was formed in 1840 in Albany, New York. Its candidate for the presidency in 1840 was James G. Birney of Huntsville, Alabama. A former slave owner himself, Birney had come to despise slavery and had campaigned in Alabama for abolition before being driven from his home. He and the incumbent Democrat Martin Van Buren lost the election to the Whig candidate,

Previous pages: a political cartoon depicts the United States Senate Chamber at the end of Henry Clay's speech defending slavery. Above the Mason-Dixon line, which is shown running through Clay's head, Clay curses the institution of slavery, while below the line he states that he will never favor any emancipation plans.

Through her novel Uncle Tom's Cabin, *Harriet Beecher Stowe (left) was successful in persuading huge numbers of people to support abolition.*

Harriet Beecher Stowe writing in her home. From 1873 until her death in 1896 she lived in Hartford, thought of as a saint by fellow abolitionists.

CHAPTER FIVE

Harriet Beecher Stowe and her brother, the noted preacher Henry Ward Beecher. Harriet was closely related to seven preachers: her husband, her father and her five brothers.

William Henry Harrison. In the 1844 election, Birney opposed the annexation of Texas, while James K. Polk, the Democratic candidate, was strongly in favor. Henry Clay, the Whig candidate, made no pronouncement for or against, and when Polk was elected, President John Tyler, who had become president after Harrison's death, saw the election outcome as a sign of the country's stand for annexation. On February 27, 1845, Tyler and his secretary of state John C. Calhoun, pushed a resolution for annexation through Congress.

In Massachusetts, the question of the annexation of Texas strengthened the abolitionist camp. Massachusetts Whigs rallied behind Charles Sumner and the "Conscience Whigs" or behind Robert C. Winthrop who favored expansion. When Polk sent troops to the area of Texas claimed by Mexico, Mexico declared war on April 23, 1846. Peace came two years later, and the United States received land that would become California, New Mexico, Arizona, and parts of Colorado and Nevada.

In 1848 the growing rift in the Whig Party became more pronounced. The Conscience Whigs were adamant in their demand for a candidate with an antislavery stand. The others refused to comply, nominating Zachary Taylor as the party's candidate. The Conscience Whigs walked out.

The Democrats, too, were splitting. When Senator Lewis Cass of Michigan (a native of Exeter, New Hampshire) was named the party's candidate as a concession to the South, the radical Democrats walked out. They called a convention in Buffalo that August, creating the Free Soil Party with the slogan "Free Soil, Free Speech, Free Labor, and Free Men." Martin Van Buren was the new party's candidate for president. Many former members of the Liberty Party and of the Conscience Whigs joined the new party. However, although the Free Soilers were successful in local elections, they could not push Van Buren into office: the Whigs carried the election with Zachary Taylor.

The enforcement of the Fugitive Slave Bill

After the Civil War, the presence of Union troops was necessary in the South to protect freed blacks from angry Southerners. An 1868 woodcut depicts a mob of whites threatening a group of blacks who are protected by the steady hand of a Union soldier.

Left: an 1880 political cartoon depicting President James A. Garfield as a friend to freed blacks. Cartoonist Thulstrup captioned his work: "Now that we have made them free, we will stand by these black allies ... until the sun of liberty shall shine with equal ray upon every man, black or white, throughout the nation."

Throughout the South, defeated Southerners attempted to "persuade" freed blacks to vote for the Democratic ticket, while Northern carpetbaggers tried to capture their votes for the Republicans. Facing page: a cartoon entitled "Of Course He Wants to Vote the Democratic Ticket."

created furor in the Northern states. Part of the Compromise of 1850, the bill gave slave owners the right to pursue and reclaim slaves who had run away. The law did not give the accused runaways a trial by jury, nor was their testimony heard by the federal commissioners appointed to adjudicate such matters. Those who concealed runaways, or law officials who refused to arrest the fugitives, were subjected to steep fines, imprisonment, and claims of civil damage.

Daniel Webster, of Salisbury, New Hampshire, became the target of much anger among abolitionists. Earlier he had argued against the expansion of slavery, but now, in order to preserve the Union, he favored the Fugitive Slave Bill. After President Taylor died on July 9, 1850, Millard Fillmore succeeded him. Fillmore backed the Compromise of 1850, and when Webster came out in support of the bill, New England abolitionists cursed him for his defection. Because of his change of heart, Webster failed in his bid to gain the Whig Party's nomination in 1852. The Whigs chose General Winfield Scott instead. The Democrats nominated Franklin Pierce, a New Hampshire Senator, for the presidency.

John Parker Hale from New Hampshire and Hannibal Hamlin from Maine were among the few abolitionists in Congress. For his condemnation of slavery and his opposition to annexing Texas as a slave state, Parker lost the support of the Democrats in his state. The few who remained in his camp joined the Free Soil Party. They had successfully campaigned to put Parker in the Senate, and in 1852 they nominated him for president. This New Hampshirite would lose to another – Franklin Pierce.

Webster's support of the Fugitive Slave Bill spurred many members of the Whig Party to defect to the Free Soil Party. In Massachusetts, the Free Soilers carried the state with George S. Boutwell elected governor in 1851 and 1852. They also elected Charles Sumner to the Senate. In Boston, however, the Whigs remained in control. Many wealthy industrialists remained committed to their Southern partners.

The Fugitive Slave Bill also spurred a Brunswick, Maine, housewife to action. Harriett Beecher Stowe, who was born in Litchfield, Connecticut, wrote *Uncle Tom's Cabin, or Life Among the Lowly,* and the first installment appeared in the June 5, 1851, edition of the *National Era.* When it was published in book form in March 1852, over 300,000 copies were sold in the first year. The next year a version of the work appeared on the New York stage, with eighteen shows a week. Through her work, Stowe swung the great majority of undecideds to the abolitionist cause.

Often condemned as a "doughface" – a Northerner with Southern sympathies – President Franklin Pierce tried in vain to keep the issue of abolition at bay. In 1854, however, Stephen A. Douglas created a new controversy. The Illinois senator, who was born in Brandon, Vermont, introduced the Kansas-Nebraska Bill which called for "squatter sovereignty" – allowing settlers in the western territories to determine for themselves whether slavery would be allowed within their boundaries. Northerners, who believed that the question of expanding slavery had been resolved forever by the Missouri Compromise, were horrified at the reopening of the issue. As a result, Democrats throughout the North lost their seats in Congress, and former party members joined with the Know-Nothing Party or the new Republican Party. New England Free Soilers, Conscience Whigs, and Democrats opposed to the Kansas-Nebraska Bill flocked to the Republican Party where they rallied around one major cause: keeping slavery out of the western territories.

The passage of the Kansas-Nebraska Bill brought bloodshed to Massachusetts. President Pierce, determined to enforce the Fugitive Slave Law, called out two thousand troops to patrol Boston for violators of the law. When Anthony Burns, a fugitive working in a clothing store, was arrested by the U.S. Deputy Marshall, Boston's Vigilance Committee called Thomas Wentworth Higginson and Martin Stowell to Burns' defense. Members of the committee formed an around-the-clock watch of the courthouse where Burns was held, determined

New Englanders hated the Kansas-Nebraska bill, which established, as a popular political cartoon explained, "popular sovereignty by giving every body liberty to hold somebody in slavery."

CHAPTER FIVE

Militant abolitionist John Brown was born in Torrington, Connecticut. He is most famous for the violent retaliatory massacre of five pro-slavery settlers that he led on Pattawatomie Creek in Kansas, and his unsuccessful raid on Harpers' Ferry, West Virginia, to free slaves in the area. Captured during the Harper's Ferry raid by U.S. troops, Brown was tried, convicted and hanged, and immediately revered as a martyr by fellow abolitionists.

President Abraham Lincoln wanted to avoid a civil war, but within a few days of his election, South Carolina seceded from the Union.

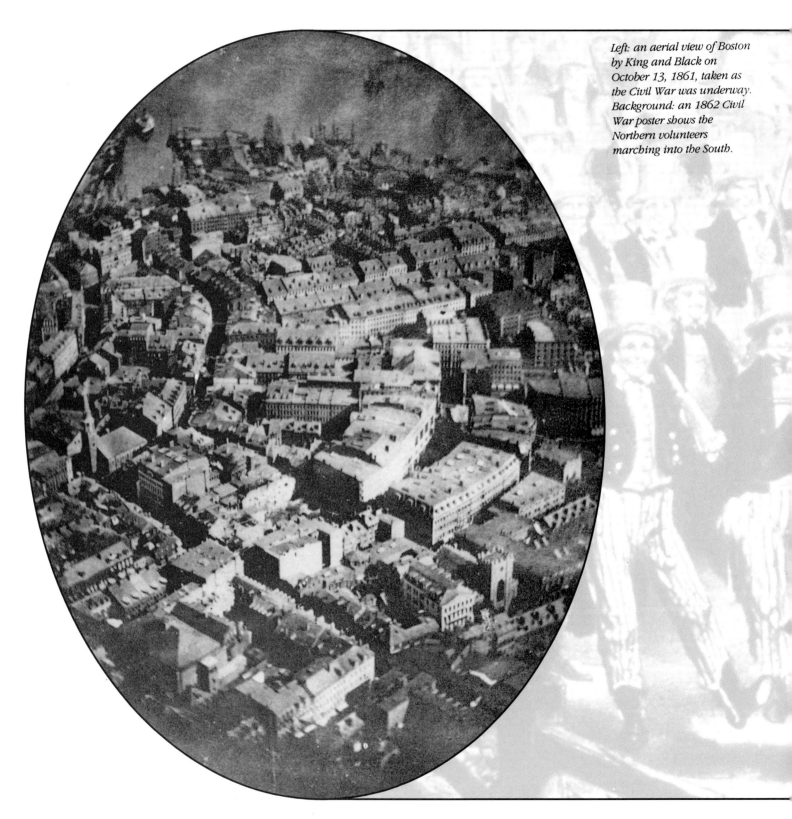

Left: an aerial view of Boston by King and Black on October 13, 1861, taken as the Civil War was underway. Background: an 1862 Civil War poster shows the Northern volunteers marching into the South.

to block his return to slavery. During a huge meeting at Faneuil Hall, the crowd took up the call to rescue Burns and rushed to the courthouse. Meanwhile, Higginson and a small band of followers who the night before had planned a rescue entered the courthouse armed with axes, revolvers, and butchers' cleavers. When Higginson heard the crowd from Faneuil Hall approaching, he ordered his band to attack. His men broke through with a beam used as a battering ram, but they were quickly surrounded by guards and one member of the band, James Batchelder, was killed. The would-be rescuers managed to escape from the courthouse, but without Burns.

In response to the Kansas bill, New Englanders created a new organization designed to keep Kansas free. The Massachusetts Emigrant Aid Company raised money to send groups of settlers to the area. Under the leadership of Eli Thayer of Worcester, the company sent its first group of twenty-nine settlers from Boston in June 1854. Throughout the summer, more groups followed and by late fall, 650 settlers were established in Lawrence, Kansas. Topeka was founded later that year by Charles Robinson of Fitchburg and Samuel C. Pomeroy of Southampton. Other settlements in Plymouth, Lexington, Concord, Osawatomie, Pattawatomie, Manhattan, and Hampden were established soon after.

The transplanted New Englanders soon faced violence when bands of Missourians tried to drive them out of the territory. In the November 1854 election, Missourians flocked into Kansas to vote for a delegate to Congress and succeeded in electing a person of proslavery sentiments. The next spring, Missourians again voted in the Kansas elections for a territorial legislature, which made its first order of business the passage of laws protecting slavery and banning abolition movements. Antislavery settlers held elections of their own, and in January 1856, two governments were posed against each other.

Political rhetoric and the settling of Kansas by people who believed in abolition were not enough

CHAPTER FIVE

An 1861 Winslow Homer engraving showing members of a sewing circle making havelocks for the Union volunteers.

for the determined New Englanders. A group of well-known men of the region came to the support of John Brown in his militant stance against slavery. Born in Torrington, Connecticut, in 1800, Brown was raised in Ohio. From a poor family, he drifted west as an unsuccessful farmer and sheep raiser. Consumed by his belief in the evil of slavery, Brown and a small band massacred five proslavery settlers on Pattawatomie Creek in Kansas in May 1856. Later, he encountered a company of Missouri Ruffians marching on Osawatomie. His band of forty men killed, wounded, or captured seventy of the Ruffians.

The halls of the U.S. Capitol would see bloodshed as well. After the sweeping victory of the Know Nothing Party in New England in the mid 1850s, and during the continued warfare in Kansas, Charles Sumner of Massachusetts returned to the Senate determined to end slavery. His two-day speech on the Senate floor attacked the policies of the administration and the stances of many senators

Union Defense Committees in the North distributed funds and relief to wives and relatives of Union soldiers during the war.

– especially Stephen A. Douglas of Illinois and Andrew P. Butler of South Carolina. The next day, as Sumner remained on the floor after the session had ended, Representative Preston Brooks of South Carolina, a relative of Senator Butler who was verbally attacked by Sumner, approached the senator from Massachusetts and began beating him with a heavy cane. Others witnessing the attack did nothing to stop Brooks. Sumner fell unconscious and was carried off the floor to receive medical attention. Throughout the North, citizens were outraged by Brooks' attack on Sumner, while Brooks' reputation in the South was elevated. Although he was censured by the House and resigned his seat, he was re-elected almost unanimously and returned to the House. Sumner never fully recovered from the attack, though he continued to hold one of Massachusetts' seats in the Senate until 1868.

In the 1856 presidential election, the Republican Party nominated John C. Fremont and took up the

Three officers of Company C, 1st Connecticut Artillery, at Fort Brady, photographed by Matthew Brady in 1864.

As their husbands, fathers, brothers and sons went off to war, Union women took their places in various capacities. Right: an engraving of female clerks leaving their work at the Treasury Department in Washington, D.C., after a drawing by A. R. Waud in 1865.

As Northern troops marched into Maryland, they were met with open arms by many citizens.

A Union soldier near his camp.

A wounded Union soldier in a Zouave uniform.

slogan "Free soil, free speech, and Fremont." The Democrats nominated James Buchanan, and the Know Nothings nominated Millard Fillmore. Buchanan won by a narrow margin in the popular vote.

The Kansas issue came to a head during Buchanan's administration. The proslavery settlers in Kansas drafted a constitution but refused to put the document to a vote of all settlers. Although the territorial governor did not back the constitution, President Buchanan decided to submit it to Congress and to press for Kansas' admission to the Union. Congress voted against admission. In October 1857, Kansans elected a new legislature in the first fair elections in the territory, and in a subsequent referendum on the constitution drafted by the proslavery settlers, the citizens of the territory overwhelmingly voted it down. John Brown's attacks in Kansas had spurred fund-raising efforts in Massachusetts, and a fund of $58,000 was raised for Kansas' aid in the summer of 1856. By 1858, the antislavery settlers in Kansas had written a

new constitution prohibiting slavery, and Kansas entered the Union as a free state in 1861.

After his raids in Kansas, Brown continued his militant career. He went to Boston in 1857 and became involved with six abolitionists in his most famous act – the raid on Harpers' Ferry. Samuel Gridley Howe, Thomas Wentworth Higginson, Theodore Parker, Franklin Sanborn, and George L. Stearns of Boston and Gerrit Smith of New York firmly backed John Brown. These men raised money for Brown and his band, bought guns for them, and supplied Brown's family with a house in North Elba. These outstanding Bostonians were committed to Brown's calls for action, but until the fall of 1858, they did not know that Brown had set his sights, not on Kansas, but on Virginia. Treasonous though the raid into Virginia might be, matters had intensified after the Dred Scott decision by the Supreme Court which stated that Congress had no authority to approve or disapprove slavery in any of the territories. When the Boston group learned that word of the impending raid was

John Quincy Adams (1767-1848) was relentless in the struggle to abolish slavery. After losing his bid for re-election to the presidency in 1828, Adams served as a U.S. representative from Massachusetts. From 1830 until his death in 1848, he waged a war against slavery in Congress.

BIRTHPLACE

Congress (overleaf) tried to silence Representative John Quincy Adams on the matter of abolition by instituting a Gag Rule, but day after day he persisted in reading petitions calling for abolition.

spreading among U.S. senators, they resolved to stop Brown from continuing his course of action.

Months later, Brown was ready to lead his raid. His Boston backers continued to supply him with funds, but some of them maintained their ignorance of his real plans. On October 16, 1859, Brown led twenty-two men from their camp on the Maryland side of the Potomac River into Harpers' Ferry, taking the armory and cutting telegraph wires. To free the slaves in the area, Brown sent out a small band of men to capture slave owners and hold them as hostages. By the next morning, troops poured into the town from Fredericksburg and Fort Monroe. Brown refused to retreat, and he was captured along with most of his surviving army on October 18.

Fearing reprisals by angry Southerners and extradition by the governor of Virginia, Howe and Stearns fled to Canada. Smith broke down under the pressure and soon began trying to disassociate himself from Brown's actions. Sanborn fled briefly to Canada but returned to Concord where he soon

violently resisted a Senate subpoena. Higginson remained steady in the course he had chosen to follow. He raised funds for Brown's defense and refused to testify before the Senate committee investigating the incident. On the day of Brown's execution, a huge crowd filled Tremont Temple in Boston. People wept as Ralph Waldo Emerson and William Lloyd Garrison praised Brown and his actions.

Before the 1860 presidential elections, the Democratic Party split, with Southern members nominating John C. Breckinridge of Kentucky for the presidency and Joseph Lane of Oregon for the vice-presidency. Northern Democrats nominated Stephen A. Douglas of Illinois and Hershel V. Johnson of Georgia. The new Constitutional Union Party, made up of former Whigs and Know Nothings, nominated John Bell of Tennessee and Edward Everett of Massachusetts. And the Republicans nominated Abraham Lincoln of Illinois and Hannibal Hamlin of Maine. Within a few days after Lincoln's election, South Carolina made good

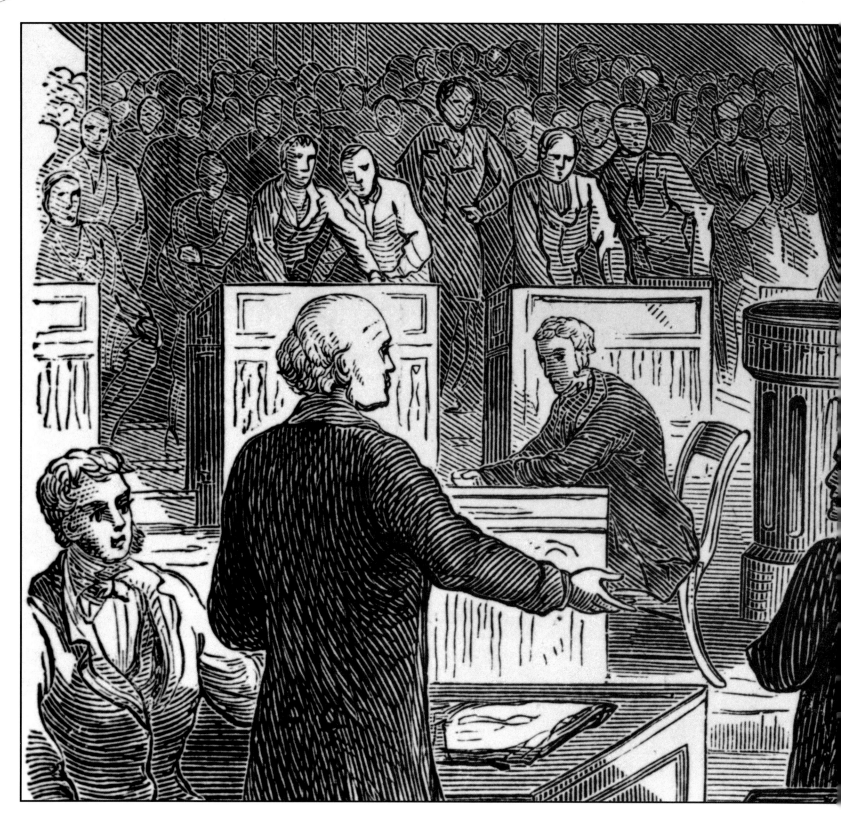

on its promise to secede from the Union if a Republican were elected president. The other Southern states followed suit, and the nation was at war.

Vermont saw only one encounter with Confederate soldiers within its borders during the Civil War. On October 18, 1864, a band of Confederates stormed into St. Albans to rob banks, and then escaped back across the Canadian border. One Vermont citizen was killed. More than 5,000 other Vermonters were killed in Civil War battles. Maine lost more than 9,000 men. New Hampshire's Fifth Regiment suffered 1,500 casualties out of 2,600 members, losses that were larger than those incurred by any other Union regiment.

While Connecticut's Union troops fought in Vicksburg, Antietam (where more than 700 members of the 16th Connecticut were killed), Fredericksburg, Chancellorsville, Gettysburg, and other battles, citizens at home formed voluntary societies to aid their soldiers. Collecting blankets, clothing, medical supplies, and food, Connecticut citizens of the Civil War period acted as they had during the Revolutionary War – when Governor Jonathan Trumbull provided essential supplies to Washington's troops at Valley Forge and Morristown. Other voluntary societies aided the families of soldiers who had been killed, or ministered to sick troops – either traveling to the front or working at Knight Hospital in New Haven.

Connecticut also contributed arms to the war. The Colt Armory, Winchester Arms Company, Christian Sharps' Rifle Company, and a host of other smaller manufacturers, all produced ample firearms for the Union Army. The Hazard Powder Company in Enfield, along with several smaller enterprises, produced so much gunpowder that Hartford County became the center of such activity in the state. Textile mills throughout New England produced uniforms and blankets, despite the shortage of cotton.

While Northern abolitionists believed they were fighting over the issue of slavery right from the beginning of the war, not until 1863 did the federal government validate that cause. Lincoln's

Emancipation Proclamation set free all slaves residing in the South as of January 1, 1863. A further step toward freedom occurred when Secretary of War Edwin Stanton reversed the United States' policy of barring blacks from military service. The governor of Massachusetts formed a black regiment – the Massachusetts 54th.

After four long years of fighting, the war ended with Robert E. Lee's surrender to Ulysses S. Grant at Appamatox on April 9, 1865. New Englanders had been among the thousands of Unionists who had given their lives to preserve the Union. In addition, they had achieved the abolition of slavery with the ratification of the Thirteenth Amendment. Along with their victory, however, came sectional bitterness and hatred more virulent than ever before.

The end of the war cleared the way for a renewed effort by women's suffrage supporters. Although the cause had generated support before the war, the exigencies of abolition and the resulting Civil War delayed any lasting effects. Throughout the country, women held subordinate positions to men, and laws governed their rights to hold property and money. In Connecticut, for example, married women were not allowed to collect the wages they earned until 1846, or to own property until 1877.

In the colonial years, there was a shortage of women, and because of the shortage, the status of women was somewhat higher than in later years. Among the Puritans, women were encouraged to work not only in their homes where they produced nearly everything their families needed, but also in the community as butchers and silversmiths and as managers of mills, taverns, and shops. But within the hierarchical society, it was the man who determined the family's position. Women were merely extensions of their husbands or fathers.

By 1840, American society had fully swung to democracy. States removed property requirements for voting, and immigrants were enfranchised. Anyone, or any man, could improve his lot by hard work, but the status of women had fallen. They were no longer encouraged to work outside the

After the Civil War, race relations in the South were extremely volatile. Two blacks accused of murder were burned at the stake near Omega Landing, Mississippi. Previous pages: a woodcut of the incident made in 1868.

Left: an 1890 meeting of women's rights activists. In that year, the National Woman Suffrage Association and the American Woman Suffrage Association joined forces as the National American Suffrage Association.

In the fight for women's suffrage, delegation after delegation of advocates appeared before Congressional committees to present their case. Right: a suffrage supporter reads her statement before the Judiciary Committee of the House of Representatives in January 1871. Below right: a meeting of the National Woman's Suffrage Association in Chicago in 1880. Susan B. Anthony of Adams, Massachusetts, and Elizabeth Cady Stanton were leaders of the organization that fought not only for women's suffrage but also for reform of the divorce laws and improved working conditions for women.

Overleaf: Victoria Claflin Wooahull of Homer, Ohio, demands voting privileges at the polls, from an 1881 sketch by H. Balling. Woodhull opened a stock brokerage company in New York City, published the Woodhull and Claflin's Weekly, and was a popular speaker on reform issues.

home, and the jobs they did have in large numbers – primarily mill work – brought them low wages. The only jobs that society approved of for women were nursing, teaching, and industrial work. Even low-paying industrial jobs did not last long for women. Irish immigrants who came to New England by the thousand replaced women as the primary work force in factories.

Well-educated upper- and middle-class women gained experience in political action working for abolition and other reform movements, such as temperance and peace. In Boston, Margaret Fuller led socially prominent and intellectual women in examinations of women's rights and other issues through her "Conversations." From these weekly discussion groups, Fuller expanded on her ideas. She wrote "The Great Lawsuit: Man versus Men, Woman versus Women," which she published in the *Dial*, the transcendentalist magazine she edited. Her book, *Woman in the Nineteenth Century,* was published two years later, in 1845, and was widely acclaimed by women's rights advocates everywhere.

In 1848, the first women's rights convention met at Seneca Falls, New York. There, Elizabeth Cady Stanton, a former resident of Boston, read her "Declaration of Sentiments," and participants in the conference protested against laws that forbade women's equality. The only demand that Stanton made that was not approved by the convention was for women's suffrage. After the Seneca Falls meeting, biannual conventions on women's rights met in many states.

One of the early suffrage workers was Lucy Stone, born in 1818 at West Brookfield, Massachusetts. Stone was raised in a devout Congregationalist family, but as a teenager she began questioning the religious doctrine that called for women's submission to men. After graduating from Mount Holyoke Female Seminary in South Hadley and from Oberlin College in Ohio, Stone began her public speaking career, first in the cause of abolition under the auspices of William Lloyd Garrison's American Antislavery Society. After a short time on Garrison's lecture circuit, she turned

CHAPTER FIVE

Margaret Fuller of Cambridgeport, Massachusetts, was the first editor of The Dial, *a transcendentalist publication. She also wrote for the* New York Tribune *and worked tirelessly for women's suffrage. In 1845, she published* Woman in the Nineteenth Century, *a book that was widely acclaimed by women's rights advocates world wide.*

"The Death of Margaret Fuller, Shipwreck of the Elizabeth." In 1847, having settled in Italy, Margaret Fuller married an Italian, Giovanni Angelo, Marquese Ossoli. Traveling back to America in 1850 from Italy, she, her husband and her son were all, tragically, drowned when their ship was wrecked off Fire Island, New York.

CHAPTER FIVE

The path-breaking work of Susan B. Anthony continued to inspire women's suffrage supporters. In a 1916 photograph, members of the National Woman's Party display a banner carrying a quotation from Anthony: "No self respecting woman should wish or work for the success of a party that ignores her sex."

As America prepared to enter the war in Europe in 1917, women's suffrage supporters picketed the White House to demand liberty for twenty million women.

Suffrage leader Carrie Chapman Catt, elected president of the National American Woman Suffrage Association in 1900 and 1915, leads a women's rights parade in New York.

Women from the middle and upper classes (facing page) worked fervently for suffrage. Poorer women had little spare time to devote to the campaign; they were busy working in sweatshops and running their households on meager resources.

Right: a courageous suffrage supporter addresses a predominately male crowd. Demonstrations and parades in favor of female suffrage occurred throughout the United States during the early twentieth century.

CHAPTER FIVE

Margaret Sanger, a pioneer in birth control education, was tried for sending her newsletter, The Woman Rebel, out through the mail. The publication was banned in the United States for being "obscene," but Sanger continued her work regardless of all sorts of harassment, helping to found the International Planned Parenthood Federation in 1946. Left: Margaret Sanger in a top hat.

her attention back to the issue of women's rights, becoming a leader in the National Women's Rights Convention in Worcester in 1850. Living in Boston from 1869 to the end of her life, she led the American Woman Suffrage Association and published with her daughter Alice Stone Blackwell, the *Woman's Journal,* which was the premier publication on women's rights.

Pauline Wright Davis of Rhode Island helped organize the National Women's Rights Convention in Worcester. She too began her career in the abolition movement, but soon grew dissatisfied with the male-dominated organizations. In 1853, she began publishing *Una,* a women's rights newspaper, and after the Civil War she served as president of the New England Woman Suffrage Association, a post she held until 1870.

After the Civil War, the movement split into two factions: the National Woman Suffrage Association under the leadership of Susan B. Anthony and Elizabeth Cady Stanton, and the American Woman Suffrage Association led by Lucy Stone. The two

groups differed in their reactions to the Fourteenth Amendment, which gave voting rights to black men but not to women. Anthony and Stanton's followers were furious that the amendment did not enfranchise women. But they directed their attention not only to suffrage but also to divorce reform and the conditions of working women. Stone concentrated the efforts of her organization on suffrage.

In 1890, the two organization joined forces under a new name: the National American Woman Suffrage Association. By keeping the issue of women's rights always in the forefront of political discussion through petitions, memorials, addresses, and conventions, the strengthened organization succeeded in its aim when the Nineteenth Amendment was ratified in 1920.

Suffragists saw the end of their long struggle to obtain voting rights for women come into view on June 6, 1919, when the bill that called for women's suffrage passed Congress. Another year would go by before enough states ratified the amendment to make it law.

THE CHANGING NEW ENGLANDER

Facing page: an 1875 engraving of fishermen hauling in their catch of herring.

Ethnicity was inseparable from politics in southern New England in the late nineteenth and early twentieth centuries. Here, as nowhere else, descendants of nineteenth-century immigrants joined the Democratic Party to line up against the old Republican elite in a battle that would be waged until the 1930s.

Ethnic diversity began to characterize urban living in New England in the last half of the nineteenth century. By 1890, one-third of the American population lived in cities. In these new urban areas, Italians, Greeks, Poles, Russian Jews, and other ethnic groups concentrated in neighborhoods of their own. Urban problems, such as inadequate housing, poor public health, and crime attended the new wave of immigration. Sanitation, fire protection, garbage removal, and traffic were problems new to the urban dweller, but housing was the most pressing problem of all. Developers in the cities could not build apartments fast enough to keep up with the tide of

immigration. Tenements were squeezed so tightly together that little light filtered between them. Disease was rampant, and infant mortality was high. Crime was on the increase, and the prison population rose fifty percent during the 1880s.

With limits now imposed on working hours for women and children, the growing industries needed a large supply of workers. Between 1866 and 1915, a massive influx of immigrants fed the giant corporations' needs. One-third of the industrial work force was foreign-born in 1870. By the turn of the century, the work force was almost 60 percent foreign-born. While earlier tides of immigration had been from northern and western parts of Europe, the immigration during the last two decades of the nineteenth century was primarily from the southern and eastern parts of the continent. Union members were vocal in their protest against the new wave. Fearing that the Italians, Portuguese, and Russians, by accepting low wages and long hours, would undermine what little progress the unions had

Streetcars changed the face of American cities for ever. Workers were no longer restricted to working only for businesses to which they could walk. Streetcars could carry them further afield. Before long American cities would develop distinct business and residential areas. Right: the streetcar that traveled the Thomson-Houston Road in Lynn, Massachusetts.

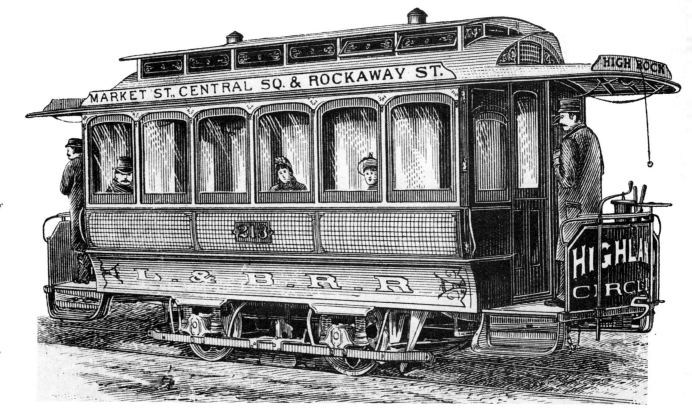

made, the native-born industrial workers were appalled whenever the new immigrants served as "scabs", or strike-breakers, for the corporate giants.

Added to the wave from southern and eastern Europe was another – from Canada. French Canadians flocked to the New England textile mills after 1870. In Rhode Island, in 1910, French Canadians numbered 34,000 compared to an Irish population of 30,000, and 27,000 Italians. About 70 percent of the state's population was foreign-born or descended from foreign-born parents by 1910, and Roman Catholics far outnumbered Protestants.

In Connecticut, immigration from the 1870s until America's entry into World War I increased significantly, placing the state behind only Rhode Island and Massachusetts in the number of its foreign-born residents. By the war's beginning, 65 percent of Connecticut's inhabitants were foreign-born. Huge numbers of Italians also immigrated to the state: in 1870 there were 100 Italians living in Connecticut; by 1900 there were 20,000. Settling in Hartford and New Haven, the Italian immigrants entered factory work, the building trades, and the food businesses. They also worked as barbers, cobblers, tailors, and musicians. With this influx of Italian immigrants, along with massive numbers of Irish, Poles, and French Canadians, Connecticut was forever altered from a rural, agricultural state to an industrial urban state.

French Canadians poured into Maine at the time of the paper industry's arrival. Farmers from New Brunswick continued to move to Aroostook County until 1870, while others from Quebec flocked to the Kennebec Valley in central Maine. From there, many Quebec natives moved to Brunswick and Biddeford-Saco, where they found employment in the textile mills, or to Oldtown and Orono where they worked as lumbermen. In the 1860s, Canadians moved into Lewiston and Westbrook. Descendants of these French Canadians numbered 77,000 by 1900, and made up nearly 70 percent of the textile mill work force at that time.

The paper industry came in full force to northern New England during the last thirty years of the nineteenth century, spawning a growth of urban areas, including that of Bath, Maine, which was serviced by the Carlton Bridge. Photograph by Lee L. Abbot.

Nativism, which had died out with the Know Nothing Party before the Civil War, sprang to full force again, striking primarily at Catholics. The American Protective Association, founded in 1887 in Iowa, worked to attack the "Catholic menace." A Connecticut chapter of the APA was formed during the depression of the 1890s, when competition for jobs was intense. In all, as many as 25,000 Connecticuters belonged to the organization, but although the group managed to control the Republican Party in Bridgeport, New Britain, and Greenwich, it did not have many followers in rural areas.

The character of urban life changed during the eighties and nineties, not only because of the large numbers of new immigrants but also because of technological advances as well. Cobblestones, wood blocks, and later asphalt paved the streets, which were lit with gaslights, electric arc lights, and then incandescent lamps. Elevated steam railways and, later, electric trolley cars took city workers to their

places of employment. People were no longer limited to employment in neighborhoods within walking distance of their homes. Development spread six miles or more from the city's center.

The combination of urban problems – housing and sanitation among them – and the new advances in transportation allowed those who had money to move out of the cities themselves, into neighborhoods like Boston's exclusive Beacon Hill and into less well-to-do enclaves of middle-class citizens. In New Haven, Connecticut, along Hillhouse and Whitney avenues, and in Hartford along Asylum, Farmington, and Wethersfield avenues, luxurious mansions were built by wealthy entrepreneurs. Squalid ghettoes sprang up where once rich and poor had lived together. In these densely populated areas, smallpox, cholera, typhus, tuberculosis, and diptheria claimed the lives of thousands of immigrants.

The settlement house movement tackled the problems of slums head-on. London's Toynbee

A Maine farmer plowing his field, photographed circa 1905. Agriculture remained a primary way of life in parts of New England, despite the rapid growth of industry.

Hall, founded early in the 1880s, was followed in America by the Neighborhood Guild in New York in 1886 and Robert A. Woods' South End House in Boston in 1892, among others. Workers in the settlement houses helped new immigrants living in slums learn about American life and customs. They protested the rampant wave of tenement houses; they worked for laws to regulate woman and child labor; they built playgrounds, libraries, and nurseries. But the efforts of these benevolent individuals could do little to stem the tide of urban disintegration. Increasingly, reform workers looked to government to effect real change.

In the Presidential election of 1896, William McKinley of Ohio was pitted against William Jennings Bryan. Central to the contest was the debate over silver. Populists wanted silver to be coined at the rate of 16 grains of silver per dollar, while the Republicans wanted the gold standard. Democrats who remained determined to maintain the gold standard – the National Democratic Party – nominated John M. Palmer of Illinois.

Republican politicians at the national level were concerned with keeping Democrats out of office. A Massachusetts representative supplied the symbol for this cause. Waving the bloodstained shirt of a carpetbagger who had been beaten by Mississippi radicals, the congressman reminded his colleagues of the misdeeds of Democrats who had pulled the South out of the Union and warned them of what would happen to the country if the Democrats regained power. The tariff was another issue that national politicians debated. New England manufacturers, of course, continued to support protective tariffs. Several industries had advanced to the point that such protection was no longer needed to promote their growth, but whenever the question of lowering tarriffs was raised, Republicans won the day

As the wealthier members of society fled from inner cities now crowded with immigrants from Europe, political machines moved into the cities. Irish politicians helped new immigrants obtain citizenship and then expected payment in the form

Background: a farmer cultivates his field with a disk harrow in 1877.

of votes at the election booth. Middle-class urban dwellers were indifferent to the city-boss system that grew up around them. When the Irish were enfranchised through naturalization, they joined the Democratic Party. The ward system that grew up New England's cities provided patronage jobs to Irish-Americans, and gave them the means to secure street lights and other city improvements, licenses for businesses, and welfare aid for their needy.

In the 1870s the Irish vote propelled numerous Democratic candidates to victory in congressional elections. Beginning in 1881, Irish politicians were elected as mayors – first in Lawrence where John Breen used his office to put his fellow Irish-Americans in city jobs. Boston's Hugh O'Brien was elected mayor in 1884.

Massachusetts' congressmen continued to be elected from the ranks of the Republican Party until 1919. George Frisbie Hoar became a senator from Massachusetts in 1877. An old-line Yankee conservative descended from a Revolutionary War soldier and a member of the Continental Congress, Hoar supported voting rights for blacks and women, worked mightily for the passage of the Sherman Anti-Trust Act, and supported American's war efforts in Cuba. He fell from favor with many Massachusetts Republicans when he failed to support the American Protective Association and the Immigration Restriction League, and refused to back America's intervention in the Phillipines.

Henry Cabot Lodge, Massachusetts' junior senator, set out to be a historian after his graduation from Harvard in 1871. In 1879 he entered and won his first political contest – for a seat on the Nahant General Court. Throughout the 1880s, Lodge repeatedly ran for a congressional seat, and lost each time, until 1886. In 1893, he finally won a seat in the Senate, where he became the leading spokesman for restricting immigration. As a tool for holding the increasing tide of immigrants at bay, the restrictionists proposed a literacy test, and the law to enforce it passed Congress easily. Only President Grover Cleveland's veto stopped the bill from becoming law and changing forever the face of America. Lodge continued his work for

restrictionism, however, and Congress again passed literacy test laws in 1913 and 1915. Presidents William Howard Taft and Woodrow Wilson vetoed the bills.

The Massachusetts' governor's office was held by Democrats for five successive terms beginning in 1910. David Ignatius Walsh was the first Irish-Catholic governor. He served from 1916 to 1919 and then went on to serve in the U.S. Senate until 1947.

In Connecticut, the Democratic Party was left in shambles after William McKinley was elected president. Fearing that their wealth would decrease dramatically, leading Democracts had been horrified by Bryan's revolutionary ideas, and had abandoned the party in great numbers. Until the 1930s, Republicans dominated the political scene in the state, with the exception of Simeon Baldwin's successful gubernatorial campaigns of 1910 and 1912. During his administration, Baldwin established a commission on public utilities, and also pushed numerous reform laws through the legislature, including a workman's compensation law that favored the worker.

Connecticut Republicans dominated state politics from 1858 to 1930, and during this time, from 1912 to 1937, J. Henry Roraback bossed the Republican Party. The lobbyist and lawyer from North Canaan directed state politics from his office in Allyn House, a Hartford Hotel, making sure that Republicans not only dominated the governor's office but also held huge majorities in the state legislature and held the congressional seats as well. One after another, Republican governors Everett Lake, Charles A. Templeton, John H. Trumbull – all wealthy businessmen – held the governor's seat, and by cutting state taxes they ensured that businesses and corporations would find a welcome home in the state. Holding the majority of seats on the Labor Committee of the general assembly, Republicans clocked liberal labor laws on working conditions, minimum wages, pensions, and benefits.

In Rhode Island, Yankee businessmen and farmers dominated the Republican Party and state government by means of voting restrictions, despite their relatively small numbers in comparison to the

Left: the Menhaden Fishery in Maine in 1882, drawn by J. O. Davidson.

population of recent immigrants. Epitomizing the Republican hold on the state was the former grocer Nelson Aldrich of Foster. After being elected to the Providence City Council in 1969 and later serving as the Council's president, Aldrich next ran for the state legislature and served as speaker for the house. In 1881, he was elected U.S. senator, where he served as the chairman of the Senate Finance Committee. Using his position on the committee to help Rhode Island business progress, he fought for high tariffs to protect the state's textile and metal industries. While Aldrich worked on the national level to ensure that businesses and corporations were favorably treated, at the expense of labor, on the home front, Charles R. Brayton kept the state's Republicans in line.

Born in Warwick, Brayton first entered the political scene with his appointment as United States Pension Officer in Rhode Island. Later, he was appointed postmaster general of the state. These two positions brought Brayton into contact with enormous numbers of people – all the

veterans of the Civil War and everyone who sought a job as a local postmaster or clerk. Brayton used his positions to hold people loyal to the Republican Party.

Amid charges of vote-buying and investigations by the U.S. Senate, Brayton continued to run a tight ship. He escaped prosecution for election fraud because the Republican-dominated Congress was unwilling to punish such a stalwart worker for the party. Then, in 1880, Brayton was forced to resign as postmaster general after it was discovered that he had embezzled $37,000 from the post office in order to pay off a personal bank loan. Loyal Republican Party members raised money for him to repay the government; he left the state for a short time, and then he returned to take up new positions as Indian Inspector and Postal Inspector for Rhode Island.

Brayton's Republican Party maintained supremacy in Rhode Island because of voting restrictions set forth in the Constitution in 1843. By law, individuals without property could vote only if

Fishing remained an important industry in New England during the nineteenth century. Facing page: a 1854 woodcut depicting men fishing from the decks of schooners.

CHAPTER SIX

they paid a one dollar fee a week before an election. Securing promises of support, the Republican Party paid the poll tax for many individuals, thus adding huge numbers to their ranks. Foreign-born naturalized citizens were allowed to vote only if they met stringent property requirements. Added to the poll tax restriction was the dominance of rural areas over cities due to malapportionment. Providence and six other large factory towns were home to two-thirds of the state's citizens, but twenty-two small towns with under 5,000 population dominated the legislature.

In 1888, nearly 15,000 Rhode Islanders were enfranchised overnight with the passage of the Bourn Amendment which abolished the property restriction in statewide elections for naturalized citizens. Although property requirements were upheld for voters in local elections dealing with tax issues or the naming of city councils, voters in the state occasionally elected Democratic mayors and governors after the Bourn Amendment was passed. Democrat James Higgins, elected in 1907, was the first Irish-American governor elected in Rhode Island.

Brayton was not to be outdone by the amendment. To maintain control of the state, even when a Democrat held the governor's office, Republican legislators pushed through the "Brayton Act," which stripped the governorship of much of its former power and reduced the office to an honorary position.

In 1909, Rhode Island's underrepresented urban ethnic citizens made another gain over the wealthy Republicans. Progressive Republicans and Democrats maneuvered through the legislature a constitutional amendment that called for apportionment in the lower house of the legislature to be determined by population size. No longer did the small towns of under 5,000 citizens maintain a majority of seats, but still large cities were limited to no more than twenty-five representatives, and even tiny towns had at at least one representative. The state Senate, however, continued to be composed of one representative from each town or city.

Despite the Democrats' victories in the passage

of the Bourn Amendment and the 1909 reapportionment, the party was split between the urban Irish reformers and the rural members who favored low tariffs and free silver and opposed American imperialism and monopolies. At the local level the reformers struggled to pass legislation to improve working conditions and to reform election practices.

After the Civil War, Vermonters moved west in droves. The proportion of improved land in the state fell from 63 percent to 45 percent, and prices for farmland plummeted to $3 an acre. With the decrease in farming, lumbering, always important to Vermont's economy, became supreme, and paper mills dotted the landscape where once stood farmsteads. Yet Vermont remained predominantly rural, with 78 percent of its citizens living on farms or in villages of less than 2,500 people in 1900.

Farmers and lumbermen joined ranks from the time the Republican Party was founded for the next hundred years to vote Republican in every election for president, governor, senator, and congressman. Beginnning in the 1840s, a series of Republican owners of railroads held the governor's office. Then in the 1870s, the Proctor dynasty emerged and remained dominant until the mid-twentieth century.

Redfield Proctor started the Vermont Marble Company in Rutland. In 1878 he was elected governor, and in 1906 his son Fletcher was elected. Redfield, Jr., took office in 1923, and Fletcher's son, Mortimer, was elected in 1945. Political battles in the state were not between the Republicans and the Democrats; instead politicians aligned themselves with the pro-Proctor and anti-Proctor factions of the Republican Party. The Proctors' chief goals in running the affairs of the state were to limit government spending, government regulation of business, and government services.

Twenty-three Republicans and only two Democrats held the governor's seat in New Hampshire from 1864 until 1914. Lumber and railroad interests dominated the political scene, and few differences can be discerned in the GOP politicians during the period. One outstanding New Hampshire politician, however, was William E.

Previous pages: fishermen haul in their catch of herring in an engraving of 1875.

Facing page: a passenger and a ticket-collector on a streetcar.

Henry Cabot Lodge (right) (1850-1924), as a U.S. Senator from Massachusetts, proposed legislation to limit the immigration into America of various ethnic groups by instituting a literacy test. Passed by Congress, the bill was vetoed by President Grover Cleveland. Photograph taken in 1896.

CHAPTER SIX

Chandler, owner of the Concord *Monitor and Statesman*. Chandler served as a member of the national committee of the Republican Party and as secretary of the navy under President Chester A. Arthur. From 1887 to 1901, he was a senator from New Hampshire. His major contribution to the state was his work to free the state from dominance by the railroads.

Between 1870 and 1890, the Boston & Maine Railroad had worked hard to take control of the several independent railroads in New Hampshire. To take over a line, however, the B&M had to secure approval from the legislature, so the railroad developed a powerul lobby. Over the years, Chandler came to hate the domination of the B&M over the state. Examples of meddling in political affairs included B&M official Frank Streeter's attendance at the state constitutional convention and his membership of the Republican National Committee. While lobbyists for the railroad succeeded in blocking any new tax laws that would harm the B&M, in 1903 they directed their efforts toward influencing legislators on matters devoid of any relationship to the railroad – local option on the sale of liquor and approval of a horse-racing tack in Salem. With these two actions, Chandler gathered his supporters in an all-out war that succeeded in stripping the B&M of its power over state government.

Republican governors dominated the politics of Maine beginning 1854, when Hannibal Hamlin became governor. James Blaine was the leader of the Republican Party in Maine for twenty years, and both Blaine and Hamlin came within a hair's breadth of being elected president.

Like the rest of the country, New Englanders were shocked by the events of June 1914, which plunged Europe into a deadly war. On June 28, Gavrilo Princip assassinated the Archduke Franz Ferdinand, heir to the throne of Austria-Hungary. Americans' immediate reaction was that the war in Europe was no concern of theirs, but as it waged on, America was increasingly pulled into the fray. With huge numbers of immigrants, and children of foreign-born parents with direct emotional ties to the various countries of Europe, internal stresses were acutely strong in New England. Individuals of German or Austrian ancestry, and Irish-Americans – due to their particular hatred of the English – in many cases supported the cause of the Central Powers. Most New Englanders, and Americans, supported the Allies, however, and the desire for an Allied victory became strong after Germany invaded Belgium, and stronger still after the Germans sunk the *Lusitania* in May 1915, killing its 1,200 passengeg after Germany invaded Belgium, and stronger still after the Germans sunk the Lusitania in May 1915, killing its 1,200 passengeg after Germany invaded Belgium, and stronger still after the Germans sunk the Lusitania in May 1915, killing its 1,200 passengeg after Germany invaded Belgium, and stronger still after the Germans sunk the Lusitania in May 1915, killing its 1,200 passengeg after Germany invaded Belgium, and stronger still after the Germans sunk the Lusitania in May 1915, killing its 1,200 passenge Massachusetts lawyer Louis D. Brandeis to the Supreme Court.

Brandeis, a native of Louisville, Kentucky, graduated from Harvard Law School in 1877. Born of Jewish immigrant parents from Prague, Brandeis stayed in Boston after graduation to practice law and to clerk for the chief juctice of the Massachusetts Supreme Judicial Court. While minorities were pleased with the Brandeis's appointment to the Supreme Court, conservative lawmakers denounced his reform activities on behalf of minorities and labor.

With the support of some of the ranks of the Progressive Party thus assured, the Democrats rallied behind Wilson with the slogan "He Kept Us Out of the War," but peace did not last much longer. After the U.S.S. *Housatonic* was torpedoed by the Germans in February 1916, Wilson called up the National Guard, and on April 2 he asked Congress to declare war. On April 4, the Senate voted 82 to 6 in favor of the war, and two days later the House followed the Senate's lead, voting 373 to 50.

War brought prosperity to New England industries and labor. Wages rose as workers

On April 2, 1917, President Woodrow Wilson asked Congress to declare war on Germany and, in September 1917, the first draftees were shipped out to training bases. Background: a World War I recruiting poster.

A young woman sanding a rifle stock circa 1915. America began preparing for war as soon as it was instigated in Europe by the assassination of Archduke Franz Ferdinand on June 28, 1914.

236

abandoned their jobs to take their places on the European battlefields, leaving industrialists with an acute labor shortage, despite the nearly half million southern black field workers who moved north to take jobs in the industries.

The American Expeditionary Force reached Paris in July 1917, manned the front near Verdun in the fall, and then in the spring of 1918 drove the Germans back from their positions in Chateau-Thierry and Belleau Wood. In September, the American forces undertook their greatest offensive of the war, driving through the Argonne Forest toward the German Sedan-Mezieres railroad. On November 11, when the Germans surrendered, the count of American dead was more than 112,000.

Wilson's efforts to create a lasting peace through the creation of the League of Nations met with strong opposition in the Senate. Henry Cabot Lodge of Massachusetts recruited thirty-seven Republicans to declare their opposition to the League of Nations. This group wanted the question of an international organization to be delayed until after peace terms had been negotiated with Germany. As the chair of the Foreign Relations Committee, Lodge wielded considerable power among his fellow senators. In a set of proposals known as the "Lodge Reservations," he delineated the conditions under which he would agree to the United States' participation in the League. His most vehement reservation dealt with the clause in the League Covenant that called for all participating nations to protect every other member nation's territory and independence. Lodge insisted that Congress would have to pass on any attempt by the United States to provide such protection.

Lodge managed to unite three factions of senators opposed to the League in varying degree – the extremists who opposed the League in any form, the mild reservationists who wanted only to alter the concept of the League in small ways, and the strong reservationists who would accept the League only if they were assured that American sovereignty would be protected. President Wilson, due in part to his hatred of Lodge and in part to his ill health, was unwilling to compromise. Recovering from what may have been a mild stroke, which he

suffered during the Paris Peace Conference, Wilson set out on a whirlwind tour of the United States to promote the League. On September 25, in Pueblo, Colorado, the president collapsed, and after traveling back to Washington he suffered a severe stroke. While the president spent two months recovering, Lodge maneuvered his Reservations before the Senate. The extremists, who wanted no part of the League in any form, and the Democrats, who had been ordered by President Wilson to block the Reservations, defeated the amended treaty. When the original draft was brought to a vote, it too was rejected.

Wilson hoped that in the presidential election of 1920 the people would cast their votes for a Democrat who supported the League of Nations. The Democrats nominated James M. Cox, governor of Ohio, who campaigned strongly for the League. The Republicans nominated Ohio Senator Warren G. Harding who dilly-dallied around the issue. In the election, Harding won more than 16 million votes; Cox garnered only 9 million. In these election results, Congress saw no mandate from the people to establish the Leage. To end the war with the Central Powers, Congress passed a joint resolution in July 1921.

Americans wanted what was termed "normalcy," which meant a rejection of the reform movements that had begun in the Theodore Roosevelt administration. What Americans got, however, was a severe economic decline between July 1920 and March 1922, during which unemployment skyrocketed and agricultural prices fell. Instead of normalcy, a "red scare" raced across the country as Americans began to fear unionism as a step toward a world-wide communist take-over.

While Democrats struggled to win local elections and to pass social legislation at the state level, wealthy Republicans consolidated a society of Yankee elites. Newport, Rhode Island, had been a summer retreat for wealthy southern plantation owners before the Civil War. At the turn of the century, northern industrial magnates flocked to Newport where they built palatial homes. Joining the Boston Brahmins who had summered there

With America's entry into World War I, women stepped into vacant jobs traditionally held by men, such as conducting trolleys (previous pages).

Henry Cabot Lodge (left) waged a successful campaign in the U.S. Senate to defeat President Wilson's plans for a League of Nations. Lodge and his supporters objected to a clause in the League's charter that called for participating nations to protect every other member-nations' territory and independence.

Women workers set type at a printing plant during World War I.

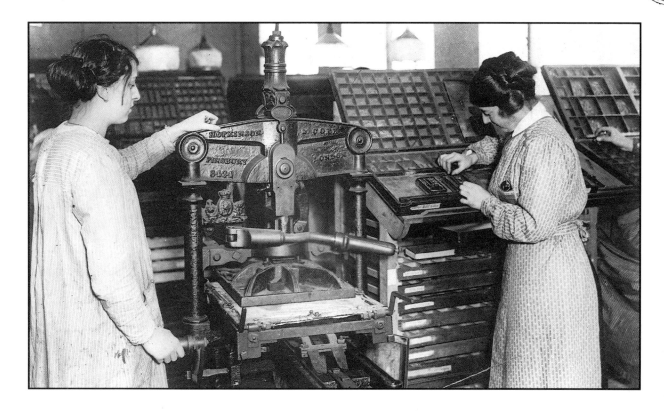

since the 1850s were wealthy New Yorkers under the influence of Samuel Ward McAllister. Creating the "Four Hundred" in 1888 – a list of New York's most socially prominent families – McAllister enlisted the aid of Mrs. William Backhouse Astor in persuading New Yorkers to spend their summers in Newport.

The way of life created by the women summering in Newport was extravagant. With budgets as high as $300,000 for the summer, the women presided over homes that were actually hotels, with as many as seventy rooms into which flowed a never-ending stream of guests. Lasting only a few years, the whirlwind Newport social life ended with the Stock Market crash of 1929. Elsewhere, resorts of less grandiose proportions continued to flourish.

In New Hampshire and Maine, the "summer people" brought new ways of life, but not on the grand scale of Newport. In the White Mountains, great hotels were built, where visitors could enjoy the splendid views of nature as well as the

entertainment and fine food provided by the management. In Maine, vacationers flocked to York Harbor, Kennebunkport, Bar Harbor, and other towns where they so enjoyed their surroundings that they returned to build summer "cottages." Tourism had come to northern New England, and the frugal-minded residents found a new source of income.

CHAPTER SIX

Vacationers (this page) in northern New England created a new source of income for the year-round residents. Tourism has became big business in the region, which offers unbounded natural beauty and a respite from urban living.

Passenger trains (facing page) took vacationers by the thousand to New England's vacation spots. Hotels and resorts were established in northern New England to cater for the "summer people" who flocked to the woods and mountains of New Hampshire and Maine.

NEW ENGLANDERS AT WORK

Logging in Maine (facing page) and other areas of northern New England was big business after 1870. The S.D. Warren Company established paper mills in Westbrook, Gardiner and Yarmouth, Maine, in the 1870s and employed people to work in three eight-hour shifts.

"Strike!" That was a word New Englanders had heard countless times between the end of the Civil War and the beginning of World War I. In 1860, shoemakers in Lynn, Massachusetts, went on strike – at that time the largest strike in American history. Following a reduction in wages, workers protested en masse in the streets, and when violence broke out, police from as far away as Boston came to the aid of the local authorities. The strike was not limited to Lynn: soon shoemakers throughout New England joined their fellow workers from Lynn in the protest. In all some 20,000 individuals were on strike. In rapid succession followed labor organizations, economic depressions, and a decline in the market share held by New England manufacturers.

In the thirty years from the beginning of the Civil War to 1890, Americans turned increasingly to industry for employment. By 1890, there were more than 3.2 million industrial workers in the country. Connecticut alone saw an increase from 5,128 manufacturing companies in 1870 to more than 9,000 in 1900. Seven million dollars worth of hats were produced each year in Danbury; $3 million worth of electrical supplies were produced in Bridgeport and Hartford; and textile mills in the state – cotton, wool, silk, and thread – produced $50 million worth of goods each year.

With advances in technology, the paper industry came full force to northern New England in the 1870s. Westbrook, Gardiner, and Yarmouth in Maine all had paper mills operated by the S.D. Warrren Company. By 1887, the company employed workers in three eight-hour shifts. While workers throughout New England were striking for better pay and better working conditions, those at the Warren mills remained loyal to the company due to their relatively high wages and the company benefits they received – including a Mutual Relief Society and a profit-sharing plan. In Westbook, owner Samuel Dennis Warren built a library, a church building, and 150 houses for workers.

Paper companies in northern New England bought woodland areas in which their workers cut trees for the hungry mills. In the 1880s, woodsmen cut spruce trees for pulp in addition to poplar trees. In New Hampshire's North Country, logging operations that had existed since 1825 were incorporated into the Berlin Mills Company, later renamed the Brown Company. By 1900 the company owned more than 360,000 acres of woodland in three states – Maine, Vermont, and New Hampshire. Much later, it controlled more than 3.75 million acres in the three states plus Canada. Workers of the Brown Company lived in camps at the site of their logging operations. After cutting trees by hand, the loggers rolled the logs onto horse-drawn skids which carried the logs to the nearest water. Most North Country logs were floated down the Androscoggin River to Berlin, whose 8,000 residents in 1897 came mainly from French Canada, Norway, Germany, and Russia.

At the turn of the century, small paper companies were no longer prevalent, the majority having been bought out by large corporations. The International Paper Company, founded in 1897,

Membership numbers of the Knights of Labor grew rapidly in the 1880s. The organization demanded an eight-hour day for its members, including both skilled and unskilled laborers. Right: a charter issued by the Scranton, Pennsylvania, chapter of the organization.

CHAPTER SEVEN

Workers in the American sewing machine industry negotiating for better working conditions or salaries. By the 1870s, textile-worker unions had 300,000 members. Between 1881 and 1905, sixty-five percent of textile strikes centered on wages.

owned mills at Livermore Falls and Rumford, Maine, and Berlin, New Hampshire, along with about twenty other sites in Maine, Massachusetts, Vermont, and New York.

Elsewhere in New England, the workplace – be it textile mill, hat factory, shoe-making company, or other industrial enterprise – became increasingly mechanized. The days of close contact between managers and employees were over, and relations between the two groups became strained. Craft unions that had begun in the 1850s looked increasingly attractive to workers. By the 1870s, such unions numbered 300,000 workers as members. However, the few concessions the unions managed to wrest from industrialists were negated by the depression that began in 1873. During the first years of that depression, workers were preoccupied with keeping their jobs. Under attack from all quarters, they feared that machines were replacing them as their corporate employers grew ever larger and more powerful. Foreign-born immigrants moved into the job market at wages that

were unacceptable to American-born industrial workers. For their part, the employers sought to control their decreasing profits during the protracted deflation of 1873 to 1897 by cutting wages and increasing hours.

During the depression, thousands of New England workers were unemployed. Three thousand workers in Lynn, for example, were laid off following the Stock Market crash in September 1873. Groups of tramps, and children looking for work, drifted through the towns, and to combat drinking and stealing by these individuals, state legislatures throughout New England passed vagrancy laws.

Workers at the Ponemah Cotton Mill in Taftville, Connecticut, went on strike on April 1, 1875, protesting against the heavy cuts in pay, and management's attempt to force out the union that had recently been established in the mill. In addition, the workers were angry that the mill charged such exorbitant rates for company housing and for food in the company store. The managers

of the mill replaced the striking workers with less demanding individuals, and the general assembly began a strict enforcement of its vagrancy laws.

Before the 1860s, piecework was widespread, but the last half of the century saw the introduction of new methods of payment. Employees were paid, for example, for the number of bed legs they turned, or the number of sleeves they sewed in coats, rather than for the number of beds or coats they made. With this specialization came concern among workers that if they produced too many bed legs or sleeves, the wages they received per piece would be reduced by the managers. Early on, craft unions set limits on the wages any single member could earn in a day, much to the dismay of shop managers.

Employers in general dealt heavy blows to their workers when they tried to unionize. In many cases they held their workers in life-long debt to company stores, and many of them flatly refused to bargain collectively with their work force. But the

union spirit, which had been largely inactive since the outset of the depression, emerged again in the 1880s. The Knights of Labor, founded in 1869 in Philadelphia, grew rapidly during the decade. Demanding an eight-hour workday, and accepting as members not only craftsmen, but also unskilled workers including women, immigrants, and blacks, the Knights had a national membership of 700,000 in 1886. However, poor management and a series of poorly organized strikes created disillusionment among the group's members. When the Knights were implicated in a bombing at Haymarket Square in Chicago, in 1886, the group suffered a decline in membership that was as rapid as its growth in the early part of the decade. In its place came the American Federation of Labor, an organization that incorporated several national craft unions. Shorter hours and higher wages were the immediate goals of the AFL, under the leadership of Samuel Gompers, and between its founding in 1886, and 1901, membership had grown to more that one

Union members waged a long struggle to improve working conditions in sweatshops where workers toiled long hours for little pay.

Cramped quarters, low pay, long hours, the presence of children on the work force (facing page), and other poor working conditions were commonplace in the textile and related industries. Background: women at work finishing ties in the 1920s.

Textile workers in Lawrence, Massachusetts, went on strike in 1912. Nearly 32,000 people were employed by the textile mills in the town, and a few days into the strike 20,000 workers had left their jobs. Overleaf: members of the state militia guarding the mills.

million.

In Fall River, however, the mule spinners had established a much more effective union. In 1858, the United Operative Mule Spinners of New England formed a benevolent society that aided strikers and individuals fired for union affiliation. The group attempted to set a firm piecework rate and to arbitrate wage disputes. When the union struck in 1870, 350 mule spinners left their jobs in Fall River. Members of the United Operative Mule Spinners joined with shoemakers and other craft unions in the Knights of Labor. In the textile and shoe-making industries, the Knights established committees to negotiate the fines that managers imposed for poor quality work, and to agree the wages paid for piecework. In Fall River, Lawrence, New Bedford, and other mill towns, employers agreed to set wages according to the price they received for their goods. When market prices rose, so did the spinners' wages.

Other textile specialists attempted to duplicate the spinners' organization, but without success. Between 1881 and 1905, more than 65 percent of the textile mill strikes centered on the wage issue. Before the major strikes in Lawrence in 1894, in Lowell in 1903, and in Fall River in 1904, most strikes were small affairs, often encompassing only one mill or even one department within a mill. Finally in 1891, textile workers met in Lowell to establish a new national union that would encompass all textile workers. The National Union of Textile Workers sought a fifty-four-hour work week and higher wages, but the depression of the 1890s stymied its efforts, and textile workers again faced wage reductions.

The Knights of Labor, the NUTW, the AFL, and other labor groups pressed for reform laws, and the AFL and the Democrats in New England at this time began their long-lived alliance. Others turned not to the Democratic Party but to socialism – the People's Party, the Socialist Labor Party, and the Social Democracy of America. The socialists never had much success in New England politics, although

they did control the governments in Brockton and Haverhill briefly around the turn of the century.

Wages and hours were not the only concerns of the new unions. Another central issue was child labor, defined at the time as employment of children under the age of fourteen. The movement to curtail the employment of children was first led by middle-class reformers, but the labor unions quickly took up the cause when they realized that their members' wages were being kept down due to these less demanding employees. In Massachusetts, the legislature had passed a number of laws restricting child labor during the nineteenth century. None was effective, however, until the passing of the 1876 and 1878 laws, which prohibited children under the age of fourteen from working in factories or workshops unless they could read and write. The laws also required industries to allow children five months of schooling a year.

Unions also grappled with the issue of working hours. In the 1840s the movement to restrict by law the number of hours factories could force their employees to work began by concentrating on women employees. By the 1860s, unions and political organizations took up the cause of an eight-hour day. Massachusets passed a bill for a sixty-hour work week for women in 1874.

The years between 1890 and 1940 were important for labor. Great strides forward were made possible by increasing organization and by changing patterns of consumerism. New England, during these years, no longer dominated as the factory king. In 1890 the east produced 58 percent of the goods manufactured in the country: by 1929, eastern factories produced only 40 percent. Still, factory output tripled between 1900 and 1940, and the number of people employed in factories doubled. During these years, the AFL was the pre-eminent organization, backing strikes by a wide variety of workers including miners, railway workers, builders, meat-packers, and steel workers.

In 1902, Danbury, Connecticut, hatters struck against D.H. Loewe and Company and called for a nationwide boycott of the company's goods. The company refused to accept its workers' demands, and in fact took an aggressive step: it sued the 250 striking workers under the terms of the Sherman Act, which mandated that individuals involved in conspiring to restrain interstate trade were liable for triple damages incurred by the company. Litigation of the case dragged on until the U.S. Supreme Court decided in 1908 that the strikers were guilty of conspiracy to restrict trade by calling for a boycott and were therefore liable for damages. The case was significant to the growing union movement because of the Supreme Court's decision to hold union members accountable for the actions of their organizations. Because of the decision, labor unions and national labor organizations began to fear that any attempts they made to improve their members' working conditions or wages would be labeled conspiracy by the courts.

In 1904, during the Danbury litigation, many unions across the country expressed dissatisfaction with the AFL. Citing the AFL's division of labor into classes of skills and its failure to recognize the deleterious effects of mechanization on the worker, and labeling it out of touch with the realities of the struggle between the working class and the capitalist class, 200 delegates met in Chicago in June 1905 to begin the creation of one big union. The resulting organization, the International Workers of the World, divided all labor into industrial unions in thirteen departments, such as the mining department, the engineering department, the textile and clothing industries department, and the transportation department.

The IWW differed from the AFL not only in the types of unions and organizations it created but also in the type of person it recruited. The AFL had long been active in trying to limit immigration to America by people from southern and southeastern Europe. The IWW, however, became the voice for workers from these countires, and it established a foreign-language press to help draw the foreign-born worker into the organization. The IWW did not want to distinguish between skilled and unskilled workers. Instead, all workers were lumped into one of the thirteen industrial

departments, no matter what specific job they did. The IWW organized textile workers into unions between 1908 and 1914 with success in Woonsocket, Rhode Island, Lawrence, New Bedford, and Lowell, Massachusetts. Skilled textile workers had previously organized themselves into the United Textile Workers, which was an affiliate of the AFL. Unskilled workers, however, had no recourse to the horrendous treatment they received from factory owners and managers until the IWW moved in to organize them.

New England metal workers also organized themselves into IWW unions. On July 15, 1907, 600 workers at the American Tube and Stamping Company in Bridgeport, Connecticut, went on strike when the company changed its policy governing night-shift workers. After the company's president threatened to close the plant permanently, more workers joined the strike. Resolution was reached only after the company agreed to resume its original plan for alternating day and night shifts, to negotiate wages, and to dismiss the plant's anti-union foreman.

Employers took drastic measures against workers affiliated to the IWW. In January 1907, the Marston Worsted Mills in Skowhegan, Maine, dismissed twenty-six weavers who were members of the IWW, and on January 21, the entire staff of 225 walked out in protest. IWW officials used the strike to address some other pressing issues. In addition to demanding the re-employment of the twenty-six sacked weavers, the IWW called for the company to eliminate its system of fining employees for inadequate work, to fire the overseer of the finishing room, and to meet with an employees' commitee to hear their grievances and negotiate on further problems. The strikers returned to work in the spring, victorious over the company.

In 1912, Lawrence, Massachusetts, was the scene of a huge strike by textile workers. At that time, twelve mills in Lawrence employed nearly 32,000 people, mostly immigrants from Italy, Greece, Portugal, Russia, Poland, Lithuania, Syria, and Armenia. The environment in which these individuals worked was intolerable: they received

After Annie Lapezzio was shot during the Lawrence strike, workers collected in the streets for her funeral, and the state cavalry (previous pages) made a show of force in the street. When the strike organizer from the International Workers of the World was arrested as an accessory to the murder, the strikers called in "Big Bill" Haywood to direct their efforts.

Nicola Sacco and Bartolomeo Vanzetti were arrested for the robbery of the L.Q. White Shoe Company's pay truck and the murder of the paymaster in Brockton, Massachusetts, on May 5, 1920. They were tried and convicted. Facing page: the two men on their way to receive their sentence. Background: violence at a silk mill in Lawrence, Massachusetts, in 1919.

poor wages, averaging around $8.75 per week; they worked under abysmal conditions; and they lived in horrid company housing that cost them approximately $2.75 per week. Tuberculosis was so widespread that in 1912 the Department of Health stated that approximately 800 people suffered from the illness in Lawrence. Most heads of households working in the Lawrence mills were accompanied to work not only by their wives but by their children as well: in fact half the children between the ages of fourteen and eighteen worked in the mills.

The Lawrence strike began after a Massachusetts' law mandating a fifty-four-hour week for women and children went into effect in January 1912, and mill owners reduced wages from the already pitifully low $8.76 per week. Workers were also angered by a newly initiated bonus system, which awarded money to workers whose output exceeded a set standard. Basically, workers in the mills saw the system as a means by which the factory owners were trying to get more work out of them for no more money. In addition, workers were opposed to the factories' system of grading output, a system devised when the Massachusetts legislature outlawed fines for imperfect work. The system involved paying workers at two different rates: one for fine cloth, the other for inferior goods.

On January 10, 1912, nearly a thousand Italian workers met to vote on the course of action they would take. They decided that on January 12, they would strike if their pay was reduced to reflect the change from a fifty-six-hour week to a fifty-four-hour week. The next day, 1,750 weavers at the Everett Cotton Mill and 100 spinners of the Arlington Mills left their work stations.

On the morning of January 12, Italian workers at the Washington Mills discovered that their wages had indeed been reduced. The workers moved throughout the mill, racing from one room to the next to shut down operations. They stopped motors, cut machine belts, smashed lights, and

pulled other workers from their stations. Half an hour later, work at the mill had completely stopped. Shouting the slogan, "Better to starve fighting than to starve working," the workers rushed out of the plant toward the other mills in town. One by one, the mills shut down. By Saturday night, the 20,000 striking textile workers had demanded a 15 percent wage hike and double pay for overtime work.

The strikers called in an IWW official, Joseph J. Ettor, known as "Smiling Joe," to help them mediate their wage disputes. Ettor was enormously successful in organizing the strikers, who represented twenty-five different nationalities and who spoke forty-five different languages or dialects. Ettor determined that each nationality represented in the work force would have a single vote in the affairs of the strike. He also formed subcommittees to deal with problems of relief, finance, publicity, investigation, and organization.

The day after the strike began, the state militia poured into Lawrence. Protecting the mill workers who remained on the job, the militia managed to reopen some of the mills. To draw more attention to the strike, Ettor organized a parade. At some point during the event, but a good distance away, a woman was killed. The police arrested Ettor as an accessory to murder. The IWW and the strikers then called in "Big Bill" Haywood to manage the strike, which continued on through the winter. In March, the mill owners acquiesced to the strikers demands, and not only in Lawrence, but throughout New England, textile workers were given pay raises.

At the time of America's entry into World War I, citizens across the country began to fear organized labor because of its radical fringe. In the American mind, the enemy was first Germany, then immigrants of Germanic descent living in America, then the Irish who seemed to sympathize with Germany because of their long-lived hatred of the British. The United States Government passed a series of laws aimed at curtailing criticism of the war. These included the Espionage Act of 1917,

*Bartolomeo Vanzetti (left)
and Nicola Sacco (right) in
court. Their trial and
subsequent appeals lasted
from 1921 until 1927 and
became an international
cause celebre.*

which punished individuals for interfering with draft laws, and the Sedition Act of 1918, which punished individuals who worked to obstruct bond sales and army recruitment and who spoke or wrote against the United States Government.

The Socialist Party, which had stated its firm opposition to the war and had determined to fight conscription and bond selling, was the first organization to be attacked by the government. In September 1917, Department of Justice officials confiscated literature and records and arrested Socialist Party leaders throughout the country. The IWW was the government's next target, because IWW leaders had published material accusing the government of engaging in a capitalist plot by entering the war. Department of Justice agents raided IWW headquarters throughout the country. At the end of the raids, Bill Haywood, the members of the IWW executive board, and everyone else who had served in a leadership capacity in the group were arrested.

Two years later, the "red scare" raced across the country. The hysteria was attributable to events in Russia and elsewhere. Americans had learned of the communist gains in Russia and of the organization's plans to spread communism throughout the world. Revolutions in Finland, Hungary, and Bavaria further fed Americans' fears. Many citizens now believed that the communists would soon wage an all-out campaign in America.

When the Boston police went on strike in September 1919, citizens throughout the country fell prey to the scare tactics employed by the press. They feared that every city in the nation would suffer under similar strikes, and even worse violence and looting. The Boston police force, largely composed of men of Irish descent, struck because the city refused to accept a police union that was affiliated to the American Federation of Labor. City officials recruited volunteer policemen from the middle-class and upper-class suburbs, and these men, together with the National Guard, called out by Governor Calvin Coolidge, restored order within three days.

The public was outraged by the Boston police

strike, and those that followed at steel companies in Pennsylvania, Ohio, Indiana, and Illinois. Before long, the press demanded that labor radicals be purged. A. Mitchell Palmer, attorney general under President Wilson, undertook the "red hunt" in August 1919, and the Justice Department, headed by J. Edgar Hoover, began collecting information about the radicals. In November, the Department leaders arrested 650 people allegedly associated with the Union of Russian Workers, which had chapters in a dozen cities. From these arrests, only forty-three people were deported, yet Palmer's appetite for "reds" increased. He ordered the issue of 3,000 warrants, and on January 2, 1920, Department of Justic agents and local police took 6,000 individuals into custody in thirty-three cities. Concentrating particularly in the industrial towns around Boston, for years the scene of great industrial battles, the raids culminated in the arrest of about 2,500 people. Those captured were chained together in groups of four and were marched through the streets of Boston. After the raids and subsequent trials, about 550 people were deported from the United States.

Attorney General Palmer continued his "red hunt" during the spring of 1920. He feared that the communists had planned massive demonstrations in cities across the country on May Day. Police forces in large cities and federal troops were prepared to fight the terrorists, but no demonstrations occurred.

But the scare was not over. On May 5, Bartolomeo Vanzetti and Nicolo Sacco were arrested in Brockton on suspicion of murder and the robbery of the L.Q. White Shoe Company's pay truck. Vanzetti, an immigrant from Villafalleto in the Piedmont region of Italy, had arrived in New York in 1908. After working in several New York restaurants he moved to Plymouth, worked for the Cordage Company, and was particularly active in a strike against the company. Blacklisted in the town because of his radicalism, he became a fish vendor. Sacco, an immigrant from Torremaddiore, arrived in Boston in 1908, and in 1913 he began attending an anarchist club, the Circolo di Studi Sociali. He lived with his wife and child in South Stoughton, where

he worked in a shoe factory.

Vanzetti was first tried for a robbery in Bridgewater. After he was convicted of that offense, he was tried, during the summer of 1921, along with Sacco, for robbing $15,776 from the L.Q. White pay truck, and of murdering Frederick Parmenter, paymaster, and Alexander Berardelli, payroll guard, at South Braintree, on April 15, 1920. The trial lasted six weeks and was conducted amid nationwide publicity. On July 14, 1921, the two men were convicted. Over the next six years, the case remained open through seven motions for retrial, all of which were denied. Throughout the country and even in Europe, the cause of Sacco and Vanzetti attracted much attention from left-wing groups, whose members believed that the men were victims of Americans' prejudice against ethnics and socialists.

When the final appeals were over, Sacco and Vanzetti's fate was left in the hands of Governor Alvan Fuller. The governor appointed an advisory committee to help him review the case. Heading the committee was Abbot Lawrence Lowell, president of Harvard University. The left-wing groups felt they had cause to question the appointment of Lowell; to them, he represented the smug, Yankee elite, despite his refusal a few years earlier to bow to pressure to fire a Harvard political science professor who had rallied to the cause of the striking Boston police. The advisory committee concluded that trial of Sacco and Vanzetti had been fair and proper, and the two Italian immigrants were executed on August 23, 1927. More than forty years later, Vinnie Teresa, an underworld informer, testifed that the robbery of the pay truck was perpetrated by the Morelli gang, five brothers who had moved to New England from Brooklyn during World War I. Sacco and Vanzetti remain symbols of Americans' fear run wild of change and differences.

Although Americans' fear of communist radicals and labor unions specifically began to dissipate, their xenophobia continued. Congress, reacting to the pervasive atmosphere, established a quota system for immigration. Congress declared that 3 percent of the total number of foreign-born residents of the United States in 1910 could enter each year. The total from all countries combined was 350,000. In 1924, Congress altered the quota system to allow only 150,000 immigrants each year, but the new system was based on the national origin of the entire white population of the country; therefore, more immigrants from Great Britain and northern Europe were allowed to come to the United States than from southern Europe.

Warren G. Harding served only three years as president before he died on August 2, 1923. His presidency was just long enough to taint him and his officials with the "Teapot Dome" scandal, in which the secretary of the interior, Albert B. Fall, accepted money from two oil companies in return for leases of land containing the government's oil reserves. Calvin Coolidge of Massachusetts took the helm, but his presidency can best be described with one of his own slogans: "Don't hurry to legislate."

In the 1924 election, Coolidge was pitted against Democrat John W. Davis, a compromise candidate put forward by the party members when they could not choose between William G. McAdoo, Wilson's secretary of the treasury, and Governor Alfred E. Smith of New York, a Catholic raised in the slums of New York City. The new Progressive Party nominated Robert M. LaFollette. Coolidge easily defeated the other two candidates. Al Smith would return in 1928 as the Democratic candidate, but he could not overcome the prejudice against his religion and his urban background, nor could he overcome criticism of his stance on prohibition and of his political machine. The Republican candidate, Herbert Hoover, won the election. In some ways, however, the election was a Democratic victory. Immigrant voters had strongly supported Smith, and after Harding and Coolidge's "normalcy" and Hoover's "New Era," the Democratic Party was ready to strike when the time was right – in 1932 in the midst of the Great Depression.

People viewing the bodies of Sacco and Vanzetti in a funeral parlor on Hanover Street, Boston, after their execution on August 23, 1927.

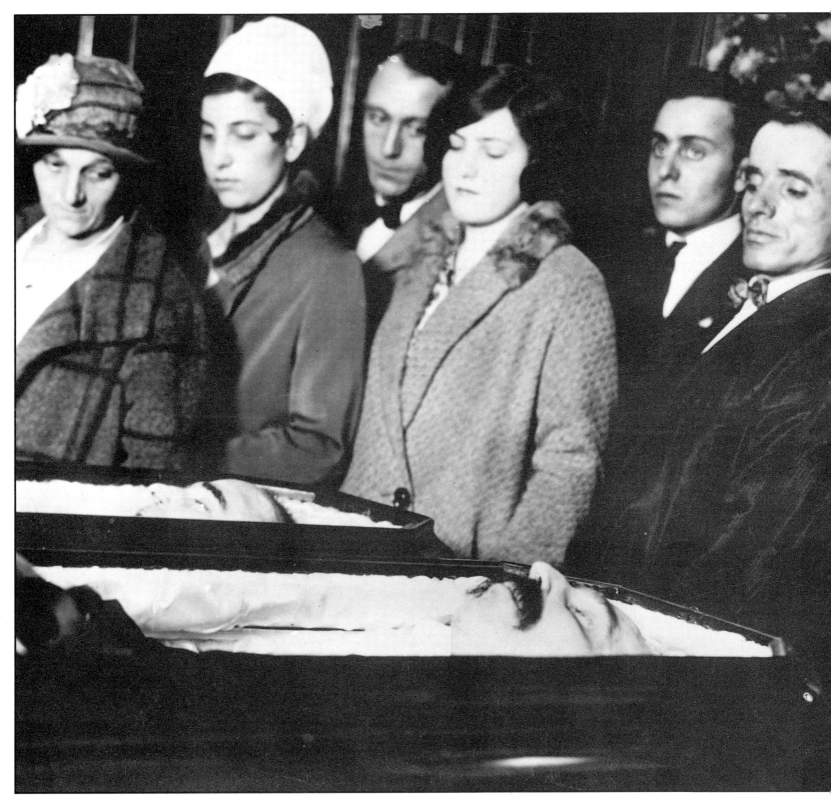

DEMOCRATIC VICTORY

Wilbur L. Cross (facing page) was elected governor of Connecticut in 1930. He was a former dean of the Yale Graduate School. He won his re-election bids in 1932, 1934 and 1936 and set the state on a firm path toward progressivism.

New England's shift to the Democratic Party began in many areas with the candidacy of Alfred Smith for president in 1928 and the Great Depression after the Stock Market Crash on October 29, 1929.

To many New Englanders of Irish and Italian descent – the largest ethnic groups in the region – Smith represented the boundless opportunities they hoped to find in America. Having escaped a childhood in the slums of New York, Smith became well known for social and welfare legislation while serving as governor of New York. Ethnic America

flocked to the polls in 1928 to cast votes for Smith and a change from the laissez faire government of the Republicans, yet even with all these new members among their ranks, the Democrats could not secure enough votes for their candidate. Another four years would pass before the Democrats would reclaim the White House.

In state elections, however, the Democrats began winning victories. Wilbur Cross's election to the Connecticut governor's office in 1930 marked the beginning of the end of J. Henry Roraback's

John Fitzgerald (right), John F. Kennedy's maternal grandfather, was elected mayor of Boston in 1905. Photograph taken in 1922.

CHAPTER EIGHT

President Franklin D. Roosevelt (left) is welcomed to Hartford by Governor Wilbur L. Cross on October 22, 1936. Cross was defeated in his bid for re-election in 1938 by Republican Raymond Baldwin. The new Governor, however, continued with many of the progressive reforms begun by Cross.

hold on the state. A retired dean from Yale University where he also served as editor of the *Yale Review*, Cross, called "Uncle Toby," was a wise politician who managed to compromise with the Republican-dominated legislature to effect real change in the state. His support centered on the working-class urban ethnic groups, and throughout the 1930s his organization gained strength. While in 1930 he had won the governor's seat by a margin of 5,000 votes, he increased that margin to 10,000 votes in 1932 and finally to 100,000 votes in 1936. During these years, Connecticut elected two Democrats to serve in the U.S. Senate and six Democrats to serve in the U.S. Congress.

Cross's program for the state included the repeal of prohibition, the creation of a program to build new schools, prisons, and hospitals, the reform of the state's banking system, and the establishment of old age pensions. He strengthened the Public Utilities Commision and reorganized state government. His tax program met with little success, however, and Connecticut was crippled for

years to come with an out-dated, inadequate system.

In the face of such sweeping support for the Democrats, the Republicans knew they would have to change, but J. Henry Roraback, the state Republican boss, held firm to his conservative convictions. As more and more Republicans swung toward progressivism, Roraback was deserted by some of his long-time followers. In 1937, during Cross's fourth term as governor, Roraback committed suicide.

Also during Cross's fourth term, scandal surrounded one of his officers. The Democratic lieutenant governor, who also served at the same time as the mayor of Waterbury, was caught with his hands in the till. Some $3 million was taken from the city by the lieutenant governor, some of the other city officials, and a number of Republican politicians. Another scandal centered around government officials who had formed dummy real-estate companies in order to buy land that was to be used by the state for Merritt Parkway. After

purchasing the land, the officials promptly sold it to the state government at a huge profit and then dissolved their businesses. In addition, $150,000 of National Guard funds disappeared at about the same time.

The Republicans used the 1938 governor's campaign to present a new-style Republican, Raymond Baldwin, as their candidate, along with promises of a new program to increase the number of jobs in private industry. Cross was hurt by the campaign of Jasper McLevey, the socialist mayor of Bridgeport. McLevey won nearly 28 percent of the vote, and Baldwin emerged as the victor with a margin of less than 3,000 votes. In his terms as governor, from 1939 to 1941 and 1943 to 1946, Baldwin continued many of the programs started by Cross, and Connecticut was firmly set on a path toward progressivism.

Rhode Island's transition from Republican-dominated state government to Democratic leaders began a few years later during the second term of Governor Theodore Francis Green. Green had persuaded the Irish-dominated Democratic Party that the time had come to open its doors to members of other ethnic groups. Backed by the new ethnic coalition, Green won the governor's seat in 1932 and was re-elected in 1934.

In 1935, Governor Green orchestrated a coup of the Republican-dominated state legislature. When the Senate met on January 1 to confirm the election of its members, as required by the state constitution, Lieutenant Governor Robert E. Quinn called for a recount of the votes cast for the two Republican senators from Portsmouth and South Kingstown. The legislature voted twenty-one to twenty to recount the votes of the two Republicans, with Quinn casting the tie-breaking vote. Upon recounting, the contested elections were found to have gone to Democrats. Next, Green and his followers reshaped the state judiciary by replacing the five State Supreme Court judges. On the bench, the legislature installed two Republicans and three

Chester Bowles of Connecticut with President Harry S. Truman (right) in 1948. Bowles served as Ambassador to India and Nepal, as a U.S. representative, and as a foreign policy advisor to President John F. Kennedy.

Democrats. With a Democratic Supreme Court, the Republicans knew any attempt to bring the legislative contests before the court would fail, and they had no choice but to accept the "Green revolution."

Green went on to purge state government of Republicans who had held office for years. He installed Democrats as state commissioner of finance, on the Providence Safety Board, and as high sheriff of Providence County. Green also pushed through legislation to reorganize state government completely, abolishing the Brayton Act that had denied any real power to the governor's office for thirty-four years. In 1936, he was elected to the Senate where he remained until his retirement in 1960. Democrats won Rhode Island's two congressional seats as well – Aime J. Forand, a Franco-American, was elected in 1936, and John F. Fogarty, a bricklayer, in 1940. Although after Green's coup Republicans occasionally won majorities on occasion in state government, many of them cooperated with the Democrats in legislative matters. Republicans held the govnernor's office only three time between 1932 and 1976: William H. Vanderbilt won in 1938; Christopher Del Sesto won in 1958, and John Chaffee won in 1962.

In Depression-era Massachusetts, the Democrats regained the governorship they had held in the 1910s, and also gained control over the governor's council. In those positions they were able to lessen the effectiveness of the cumbersomely large state legislature, dominated by rural interests, and to increase the power of a new ethnic coalition. During the 1930s, a Massachusetts expatriate, Joseph P. Kennedy, emerged on the national political scene. While living in New York, he was appointed the first chairman of the Securities and Exchange Commission and later ambassador to Great Britain, by President Roosevelt. Kennedy had broken through the Yankee stronghold on banking and finance in 1914, just two years after he had graduated from Harvard. That year he married Rose Fitzgerald, the daughter of John F. Fitzgerald, who served as Boston's mayor from 1906 to 1907. Kennedy went on to become a member of the board of trustees of the Massachusetts Electric Company and to acquire a family fortune through widely varied investments. In 1927, Kennedy moved with his family to New York, perhaps as a result of the apparent impossibility of breaking the grip of the Yankee elite society. He and his family would return after World War II.

Even Republican Maine succumbed to the Democratic onslaught in the 1930s. Four times between 1932 and 1958, Democratic candidates won the governor's seat in the former Republican stronghold.

In Vermont and New Hampshire, while the Democrats did not win elections, a new breed of Republican took control. The old-line Proctor dynasty in Vermont was bested by Warren Austin, who won a seat in the U.S. Senate. Austin angered the old-liners when he supported some New Deal measures in the Senate. In 1946 he left the Senate for a new post as the United States' chief delegate to the United Nations.

Vermont's George David Aiken emerged on the scene first as state legislator and as speaker of the house, then as lieutenant governor, and in 1936 as governor. He endeared himself to the rural interests in the state and gained the undying hatred of the Proctor organization and the public utilities. Aiken encouraged farmers to market their products jointly and to establish cooperatives for electrical service and insurance. In 1940 he defeated Ralph A. Flanders for a seat in the U.S. Senate.

Liberalism swept through the New Hampshire Republican Party with John G. Winant and Charles W. Tobey. Winant had entered political life in 1916 when he was elected to the state legislature. He introduced a slate of social reforms including laws to limit the work week for women and children, to set a minimum wage, and to abolish capital punishment. All were defeated. Elected governor in 1924, Winant introduced thirty progressive legislative issues in his inaugural address. However, while most of his proposals were made law, Winant was unable to push through a forty-eight hour bill, a child labor amendment to the constitution, and a more liberal workmen's compensation bill – the

Joseph P. Kennedy in 1956. The patriarch of the famous Kennedy clan became president of a bank in 1914 at the age of twenty-five. Later he was appointed Chairman of the Securities and Exchange Commission and Ambassador to Great Britain.

three pieces of legislation he most sincerely sought. Winant was defeated in 1926, but when he ran again in 1930 and 1932, he won. He enthusiastically supported New Deal programs and social reforms during the Depression.

As governor, U.S. representative, and senator from 1929 to 1953, Charles W. Tobey continued the liberal Republican tradition that Winant had begun.

In 1934, Styles Bridges recovered the conservatives' power when he was elected New Hampshire's governor. Bridges had served on the state's Public Service Commission under Governor Tobey and was originally viewed as a progressive. After serving as governor, he won one of Vermont's Senate seats in 1936. He surprised his state by voting along a conservative line, but because of his ability to get things done for constituents, he was returned to the Senate time and again until his death in 1961.

Throughout America, the Depression, spawned by too much industrialization and too much wealth concentrated in the hands of too few, wreaked havoc on rich and poor alike. People had no money to purchase the products being churned out by America's factories at an increasingly rapid pace. Overproduction and underconsumption combined to spur factory owners to shut down plants and lay off workers. Nearly 5,000 banks closed their doors in the first three years of the 1930s. Agricultural prices fell as well because Americans no longer had money to buy as much food they had before the Depression.

The Depression ensured that the Democrats would win the presidential election of 1932 over the Republicans, who seemed to be doing little to stave off the ill effects of the economic crisis. Franklin D. Roosevelt, governor of New York and a graduate of Harvard, was the Democratic candidate. In the election, he won 22.8 million votes to Hoover's 15.8 million. Due largely to the successes and popularity of Roosevelt's New Deal, he easily won re-election in 1936.

Throughout the country about 13 million people were out of work, and New England bore a large share of the unemployment. In Connecticut, for

example, 150,000 were unemployed – 16,000 in Bridgeport alone. By 1933, unemployment figures in the state rose another 14 percent, and the state's poor marched on the state capitol in Hartford to demand $12 million in relief for the unemployed. At first Governor Cross, stating that Connecticut's sovereignty was threatened by federal relief programs, resisted the lure of federal funds, but as the plight of urban areas worsened, he established the Emergency Relief Commission through which New Deal funds filtered into the state.

Unemployed New Englanders went to work in government-sponsored job programs that built roads, sewers, bridges, hospitals, town halls, and airports. Others took part in experiments on ways to control mosquitoes on the eastern shore. Still others painted murals in public buildings. Roosevelt's New Deal created the Civilian Conservation Corps, the National Industrial Recovery Act, the Public Works Administration, the Agricultural Adjustment Administration, the Works Progress Administration, and myriad other agencies to filter money through the states to the nation's destitute. The WPA alone spent $11 billion and employed nearly 8.5 million people between 1935 and 1943.

While America struggled to keep hunger at bay during the Depression, around the world events were occurring that would ultimately have a grave impact on her preoccupied citizens. Japan invaded Chinese Manchuria in 1931; Benito Mussolini sent Italian troop to invade Ethiopia in 1935; Spain engaged in a deadly civil war beginning in 1936; and Adolf Hitler cemented his control over Nazi Germany, annexed Austria, seized Czechoslovakia, invaded Poland, and forced France to surrender. America, hiding behind neutrality acts and arms embargoes, reached new extremes of isolationism.

Roosevelt, who sought and won a third term as president in 1940, faced a new and deadly alliance comprising Italy, Germany, and Japan. On December 7, 1941, Japan attacked Pearl Harbor. Congress declared war on Japan on December 8, and three days later, Japan's allies, Italy and Germany, declared war on the United States. By the

Previous pages: Senator George Aiken of Vermont in 1972. He served as a state legislator, speaker of the house, lieutenant governor, and governor before entering the U.S. Senate in 1940. He remained in the Senate until 1975.

Left: William Loeb (center), publisher of the Manchester Union Leader *in Manchester, New Hampshire, and outspoken conservative, receiving an award from the "Assembly of Captive European Nations."*

Kansas Senator Robert Dole, the Republican vice-presidential candidate in 1976, listens as New Hampshire Governor Meldrim Thomson speaks to the annual meeting of the Republican State Committee. Thomson became well known after his election in 1972 as an ultra-conservative spokesman for the Republican Party.

war's end, incalculable numbers of people had died around the globe, but for America, the future seemed bright. No longer isolationist in policy, Americans rejoiced in the death of Fascism and the possible containment of Communism. Participation in the new United Nations organization seemed to promise peace for generations to come.

CHANGING ATTITUDES, NEW ECONOMIES

The story of New England politics in the second half of the twentieth century is peopled by national figures. The names of Margaret Chase Smith, Edmund Muskie, John F. Kennedy, Robert Kennedy, Edward Kennedy, Thomas P. O'Neill, Jr., Michael Dukakis, Claiborne Pell, and Ella T. Grasso are familiar to Americans nationwide, not just to those in the six-state region. Their various rises to power – to the Senate, to the state capitols, and to the White House itself – are stories that reflect not only the changing temperament of New England but that of the country as a whole. The issues in which they became involved are issues that affect all Americans: declining cities, education, environment, labor, and shifting economies.

John Moran Bailey of Connecticut is one example of a New England politician whose sphere of influence stretched right across the country. Bailey served as chairman of the state Democratic Party from 1946 until his death in 1975. A graduate of Harvard Law School, he first entered politics as a precinct worker in Hartford in the 1930s. Bailey was the prime backer of such people as Abraham Ribicoff and Ella Grasso.

Grasso made political history in in 1974 as the first woman elected to be governor of a state without succeeding her husband. The former two-term congresswoman was also the first Italian-American elected Connecticut's governor, and her victory marked the total dominance of the Democratic Party in the state by Italian-Americans, the largest ethnic group. Grasso, whose full name is Ella Rosa Giovanna Oliva Tambussi Grasso, grew up in Windsor Locks and lived there for most of her life. She graduated from Mt. Holyoke in 1940. One of her primary goals as governor was to secure for her constituents a more responsive Public Utilities Commission and to reduce the cost of state government.

Abraham Ribicoff, governor and senator from Connecticut, is a native of New Bern. His early career was spent working in real estate and investing in various businesses, activities which earned him a fortune. At the age of twenty-eight, Ribicoff was elected to the state legislature, and

JOHN HARVARD
FOUNDER

Democratic U.S. Senator Claiborne Pell of Rhode Island and his wife in 1978. Pell entered the Senate in 1960 and became well known for his sponsorship of the bill that established the National Foundation of the Arts and Humanities.

John Moran Bailey, chairman of the Democratic National Committee, at the Democratic National Convention in August 1964. Bailey was appointed chairman of the committee by President John F. Kennedy.

from there he went on to become governor, secretary of HEW, and U.S. senator. He is perhaps best known for his consumer protection and safety stances in the Senate.

John Moran Bailey's largest claim to fame outside of New England is for his backing of Massachusetts senator John F. Kennedy for president in 1960. As the first Democratic state chairman to back John F. Kennedy, Bailey was rewarded by the new president with the job of national chairman of the party.

John F. Kennedy was first elected to political office in 1946 as a congressman from Massachusetts. In 1952 he won a seat in the Senate, defeating Henry Cabot Lodge, Jr, the grandson of the man of the same name who fought Wilson over America's participation in the League of Nations. In the 1960 presidential election, voters throughout the country were enthralled by Kennedy's youth and energy, electing him over Richard M. Nixon. Kennedy did not have long to carry out his vision for the country. With an assassin's bullet his work toward

civil rights, detente between the United States and the Soviet Union, assisting third world countries, and forming stronger alliances between the United States and European nations all came to an end.

Robert Kennedy, the next son in the Kennedy dynasty, seemed destined to follow his older brother to the White House. Having served as manager of his brother's campaign, as attorney general in his brother's administration, and as a senator from New York, he entered the contest for the Democratic presidential nomination in 1968 and seemed to have an excellent chance of winning. While on the campaign trail, he too was struck down by an assassin.

Edward M. Kennedy, the youngest brother, first ran for the Senate in 1962 at the age of 30, and was vying for the 1972 presidential nomination when he became embroiled in the scandal surrounding his car accident which caused the death of his secretary Mary Jo Kopechne at Chappaquiddick Island. The incident ended any hopes of becoming president, but Kennedy remains a vital force in the Senate,

Left: Robert F. Kennedy on the Capitol lawn in 1965. In 1968, an assassin's bullet ended Democratic hopes for another Kennedy in the White House.

Facing page: Edward and Robert Kennedy.

working for nationalized health insurance and other liberal causes.

Another Massachusetts senator, Edward Brooke, made political history when he became the first black in this century to be elected to the Senate. A rather liberal sort of Republican, as all Massachusetts Republicans are, Brooke served the Senate from 1967 to 1979.

Thomas P. "Tip" O'Neill, congressman from the same district that elected John F. Kennedy in 1946, became speaker of the House of Representatives in 1977. Known for his pragmatic good sense and his ability to move legislation, O'Neill had a rapport, equalled by few politicians, with his constituents, who often met with him on his Saturday walks through his district.

Michael S. Dukakis added his name to the long list of presidential candidates from Massachusetts in 1988. Dukakis served first in the state legislature, where he wrote (and steered through passage despite enormous opposition) the country's first no-fault insurance law. Elected governor in 1974 at the age of 41, Dukakis backed legislation to replace the Department of Public Utilities with a new consumer-oriented commission and struggled with the dire financial condition of state government. He instituted a program called "workfare," designed to provide jobs for fathers on welfare. In 1978, Dukakis ran for re-election and lost, but in 1982 he was returned to the governor's office. In the 1988 presidential election Dukakis waged a well-organized fight against the victorious George Bush.

Rhode Island's Claiborne Pell was born into a family of considerable wealth. He graduated from Princeton in 1940 and earned a master's degree in international administration from Columbia. During his early career, he worked in the U.S. Foreign Service. He entered politics in 1960, winning the Democratic nomination for senator with 61 percent of the vote after running an extremely well-financed campaign during which he surprised ethnic voters with his ability to speak Portuguese, French, and Italian. During the Vietnam War, Pell used his position on the Senate Foreign Relations Committee to oppose America's participation in the conflict.

Previous pages: the Kennedy clan in 1960. Seated (left to right): Mrs. R. Sargent Shriver, Mr. and Mrs. Joseph P. Kennedy, Mrs. John F. Kennedy, and Edward Kennedy. Standing (left to right): Mrs. Robert F. Kennedy, Mr. Stephen Smith, Mrs. Smith, President-elect Kennedy, Robert F. Kennedy, Mrs. Peter Lawford, Mr. Shriver, Mrs. Edward Kennedy, and Mr. Lawford.

Left: Senator Edward M. Kennedy speaking in Boston in 1968. He first won a seat in the U.S. Senate in 1962 at the age of thirty.

Governor Michael D. Dukakis of Massachusetts was the Democrat's choice for president in 1988.

For historians, artists, and other humanists, Pell is revered for his sponsorship of the bill that established the National Foundation of the Arts and Humanities.

George Aiken, Vermont's governor from 1937 to 1941, entered the Senate in 1941 and held his seat until he retired in 1975 at the age of eighty-two. Aiken was widely known for his boast that he never spent any money campaigning: instead, he spent his time getting to know the communities he served and attending to their problems. He was also known for his down-home humor and practical advice, one piece of which dealt with the Vietnam War: "The United States should declare victory and get out."

Margaret Chase Smith, from Skowhegan, Maine, won the Republican nomination for the U.S. Senate in 1948. While serving in the Senate, she set a record for the number of continuous roll-call votes cast – 2,941. Seeking re-election at the age of 74, Smith was defeated in 1972.

In 1954, the Democrats in Maine nominated Edmund Muskie for governor. The former state legislator from Rumford, Maine, waged a poorly financed campaign for the governor's seat, always spending the night on the campaign trail in the homes of his supporters, always searching desperately for money. Muskie ran very well in 1954, winning 135,673 votes to the Republican candidate's 113,298. His personality and honest government persuaded many Republicans to defect from their party. At re-election time in 1956, he won again, this time by 56,000 votes. Two years later, voters in Maine sent him to the Senate by a majority of 61,000 votes, where he remained until 1980. In 1968, he was extremely close to winning the Democratic nomination for president.

New England's economic difficulties became acute at the beginning of the twentieth century. Many of the large textile mills moved operations out of the region to the south. At the industry's peak, as many as 400,000 New Englanders worked in textiles, in cities such as Lowell, Lawrence, and Fall River, Massachusetts; Manchester, New Hampshire;

Senator Lowell Weicker of Connecticut cross-examining a witness during the Senate Watergate hearings in 1973. He was first elected to the Senate in 1971.

In September 1975, nearly 3,000 people gathered at a rally (background) held in Boston's City Hall Plaza to protest busing to achieve racial integration in schools.

Edmond S. Muskie served as governor of Maine from 1954 to 1958. He was elected to the U.S. Senate in 1956 and served until 1980.

and Woonsocket, Rhode Island. Between 1929 and 1950, as many as 149,000 of these workers lost their jobs, as mills closed their doors. By the 1970s, only 75,000 jobs remained in the industry. Much of the decline stemmed from the northern textile factory owners' unwillingness to branch out into the new synthetics that were being produced in vast quantities in the south. In addition, southern mill operatives worked at much lower pay rates than their New England counterparts, thus bringing to the southern factory owners a favorable profit margin.

One of the most disastrous plant closings occurred in 1936 when the Amoskeag Manufacturing Company in Manchester, New Hampshire, closed its doors and forced 15,000 people out of work. The closing was a huge blow to the New England textile industry, as Amoskeag had been the largest textile company in the world. The city of Manchester was crippled.

The shoe industry, dominated for years by shops in Massachusetts, suffered in the first half of the

twentieth century as well. Shoe-making had a history in New England nearly three centuries long, and the majority of national consumers wore New England-made shoes. At the turn of the century, 47 percent of the shoes made in the United States were from Massachusetts alone. In the 1920s, shoe factories opened in the Mid-Atlantic and Midwest states. Employment in the industry dropped from 145,000 in 1929 to 110,000 in the late 1940s. Foreign imports, pouring into the country in the 1960s, further crippled the New England industry. Between 1958 and 1971, 35 percent of the people employed in New England's shoe factories lost their jobs.

Ship-building, as well, has suffered, and many of New England's ports, which for centuries drew huge volumes of trade and commerce, are now in poor condition.

The economic condition in Connecticut, heavily dependent on defense spending, has suffered violent swings of plenty and want during the years since the end of World War II. Revitalized in the late 1930s and 1940s, due to America's wartime

A famous World War I
recruiting poster.

A 1923 supporter of the Harvard team.

Fishing for sport was widespread off New England's coast throughout its history.

New England beaches, especially those of Newport, Rhode Island, and Kennebunkport and Bar Harbor, Maine, were prime vacation sites for the wealthy.

spending, the economic picture bleakened at various points during the Cold War, brightened during the Korean and Vietnam conflicts, and then darkened again. Despite the swings in defense-related jobs, the number of individuals employed in manufacturing has remained relatively level—at about 400,000—since the end of World War II. In addition to maintaining its lead in the insurance field, Connecticut has diversified into other service and nonmanufacturing interests. The state continues to attract major corporations looking for new national headquarters.

Massachusetts' economy also became heavily dependent on government defense contracts after World War II. In 1946, a new firm called American Research and Development, backed by Boston financiers, started investing in new scientific industries, the first being Tracerlab. Over the years, hundreds of new companies, staffed by graduates of MIT, were begun in Cambridge. Before long, Route 128 was a major center for technology in

space, missiles, and electronics. Unfortunately, however, the profits of these high-tech companies depend on the number of contracts given to them by the federal government, which swings from high defense spending to low with every change of administration.

Rhode Island fell victim to just such swings in 1973, when the Defense Department pulled several naval installations out of the state. The Naval Air Station and the Naval Air Rework Facility had been the state's largest employers, but during that year, 3,600 employees lost their jobs when the facilities closed. In 1975, unemployment stood at about 18 percent.

In New Hampshire, in the 1960s, new industries began locating in the "Golden Triangle," the area bounded by Manchester, Nashua, and Portsmouth. During that decade more than 300 plants set up operations.

In general, however, the economy of the New England states suffers due to the difficulty in

Boston's City Hall and Government Center, photographed in 1971, was built by Kallman, McKinnel and Knowles. Background: Harvard College.

CHAPTER NINE

The woods of northern New England provide vacationers (previous pages left) with a respite from city living. Previous pages right: the entrance hall to the Sterling Memorial Library at Yale University. The University's library collection is the fourth largest in the United States.

Left: Senator George Aiken (left) of Vermont greets Secretary of State Henry Kissinger (right) at a meeting of the Senate Foreign Relations Committee in 1974. Aiken retired from the Senate in 1975 at the age of eighty-two.

attracting new business and industry. The cost of living in the area is far higher than the national average in the United States, construction costs are high, land prices have soared, and environmenal restrictions placed on industry are stiff. In addition, tax rates are higher than the national average because of the large number of social services provided by the states.

The decline of cities, and inter-ethnic tensions, are major problems in New England. "White flight" to the suburbs has resulted in inner cities plagued by crime, drug use, and shrinking city services. Connecticut and Massachusetts were the scenes of violent racial uprisings in the 1960s and 1970s. During the summer of 1967, the cities of Bridgeport, Middletown, New Britain, New Haven, New London, Norwalk, Stamford, and Waterbury in Connecticut all suffered tremendous unrest. Hartford's racial problems spread over three summers, from 1967 to 1969. Much of the tension was due to the state's failure to deal with school integration, poverty, and the dismal condition of the

inner cities. In the 1970s, Boston was the scene of violence stirred up because of court-ordered school busing.

New England is known, however, for several products and services that far outweigh the negative aspects. It is a region that is known world wide for its precision products such as clocks, rifles, and jewelry. Connecticut, sometimes called the "Gadget State," was the first home of Charles Goodyear's vulcanized rubber industry, and today the state boasts several specialized metal-working plants. All along Route 128 and into Hartford, southern New Hampshire, Rhode Island, and Burlington, Vermont, industries have set up shop to produce papers and plastics, photographic instruments, biomedical instruments, electronic components, mainframe computers and peripheral components, and missile and space systems.

New England state government has been aggressive in trying to find answers to the economic crisis. "Project Rhode Island," for example, was initiated in the 1970s by businessmen and labor

Margaret Chase Smith of
Maine served in the U.S.
Senate from 1948 to 1972.

Overleaf left: Wellesley College
Tower in Wellesley,
Massachusetts, twelve miles
west of Boston. The College
was founded in 1870.
Overleaf right: Harkness
Memorial Tower at Yale
University.

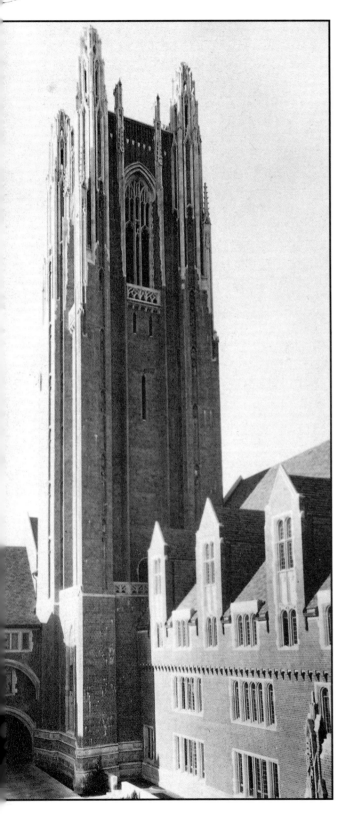

leaders to identify problems with the state's economy. One finding of the report commissioned by the group was that Rhode Island ranked in the bottom eleven states on the average grade completed by its citizens. One of the most important recommendations to come from the report was that vocational training programs needed to be installed to upgrade the labor force. The report encompassed more than education, however. It focused on land use planning, tax reform to attract businesses, wage levels in factories, and overall economic development as well.

Under Michael Dukakis, Massachusetts has regained its old economic vigor, and was touted by *Time* magazine as a "go-go state that is leading the transition to … a high-tech, service-oriented economy." Still dependent on federal defense spending, the state has profited, nevertheless, from an influx of private businesses, due largely to Dukakis' actions to improve the state's attractiveness. Between 1983 and 1985, 140,000 new jobs were created.

Ten percent of the nation's colleges and universities are located in the six-state New England region. Harvard, Yale, MIT, Brandeis, Dartmouth, Williams, Smith, Mt. Holyoke, Bowdoin, Amherst, the Universities of Massachusetts and Connecticut, Boston University, and Northeastern University all pull massive numbers of college-bound students into the area. One study by the Federal Reserve Bank of Boston showed that private universities pull more dollars into New England than any industry located there.

Tourism, too, draws money into the region. New England is an area of varied beauty and great historical interest. In Connecticut, visitors flock to Mystic Seaport, the P.T. Barnum mansion in Bridgeport, and the beautiful scenery around the Berkshire Hills. In Massachusetts, Revolutionary War sites draw huge numbers of visitors to the "Cradle of Liberty." Vermont's Green Mountains have been favorite vacation spots since the mid-nineteenth century, and the summer-camp business is a lucrative enterprise. At the peak of the tourist season in Vermont one is likely to see fifteen times

Previous pages: Harvard University as seen from the banks of the Charles River. In the early 1970s, Harvard College and Radcliffe College merged their administrative and admissions offices. Yale University (previous pages background) located in the heart of New Haven, Connecticut. Yale was founded in 1701 and more than 10,000 students are enrolled in the University. It is the second oldest university in the country. Originally named the Collegiate School and located in Branford, Connecticut, the school moved to Saybrook in 1701, then to New Haven in 1716 where it was renamed Yale College.

Facing page: a photograph taken in 1960 of the electrical engineering building at the Massachusetts Institute of Technology, Cambridge. The Soviet hammer and sickle flag was placed on the building during student protests. MIT was founded in 1861 and was originally located in Boston. Right: the back entrance to the Smith College library. The college, located in Northampton, Massachusetts, was founded in 1871. It is the largest private college for women in the United States.

Brown University in Providence, Rhode Island, was founded in 1764 through a charter from the colony's general assembly. Today 7,600 students attend the university.

The Commons Building at Bennington College in Bennington, Vermont. Founded in 1932, this small college enrolls 600 students at its lovely campus at the foot of the Green Mountains.

more visitors than natives in the state, which boasts more than forty ski areas.

But threatening the natural beauty that draws so many visitors are serious environmental problems, notably polluted water, air pollution, and over-development in formerly rural areas. The New England states have pursued solutions to these environmental problems at a rate faster and at a level more strict than in the rest of the country. The Connecticut legislature, for example, approved a water pollution act in 1967, an air quality control act in 1970, and a solid waste management act in 1972. In the early 1970s, most of Connecticut's industrial facilities were at least fifty years old, but in recent years these factories have gone through state-mandated pollution abatement programs. In 1974, Connecticut also began a pioneering $295 million recycling program.

A serious threat to New England's beauty is the huge and ever-increasing number of second homes and retirement homes being constructed in the north. In the 1960s, Vermont citizens became aware of the dangers of these proliferating second-home developments and ski areas. Haphazard and poorly executed development spread over the area, especially in southeastern Vermont near Mount Snow in the Dover area and Haystack Mountain in the Wilmington area. Land prices skyrocketed as developers vied for the choicest parcels. Near Stratton Mountain, developers were willing to pay as much as $25,000 an acre. Vermont natives suffered under huge property taxes, and many were forced to move off their land or to close their businesses because of the tax hikes.

After Vermont residents took their concerns to their representatives, the state legislature passed Act 250 in April 1970. The new law established standards for development, created local and state review boards, and pointed the way toward a land-use plan to be developed for the state as a whole. Act 250 did little to slow the pace of development, but the quality of the new development is far superior to that of earlier sites.

At the brink of America's entry into the twenty-first century, the homogenous population of New

Previous pages: the Phillips Exeter Academy in Exeter, New Hampshire, a leading preparatory school.

Left: Charlestown policemen turned out in full force to guard against violence as buses carried black students to white high schools in September 1975 – the historic Bunker Hill Monument can be seen in the background.

Amherst College (this page) in Amherst, Massachusetts, was founded in 1821 to educate young men preparing for the ministry. It became coeducational in 1975 and today enrolls 1,500 students.

AMHERST COLLEGE.

England no longer exists. Made up primarily of people from English and Scots ancestry until the mid-nineteenth century, the population of New England today is composed mainly of the descendants of immigrants from other European nations and from Canada. From Puritan selectmen to Irish and Italian ward leaders, the people of New England have evolved into a tree with many branches – all sprouting from a strong trunk of Puritan idealism and Yankee pragmatism. When New Englanders went off to fight on the battlefields of Europe and the Pacific area, they left behind many of the distinguishing characteristics that had determined sectional politics in America.

Yet New Englanders are the original Yankees, though the exact origin of the term is unknown. Some say that "Yankee" comes from the Dutch name "Janke" (the diminutive of Jan – John) which the Dutch settlers called the English. Others say it derives from the Cherokee word "eankke," a word said to mean "slave" or "coward" used by Virginia settlers to describe New Englanders who refused to participate in the Virginians' war with the Cherokees, (although no such word as "eankke" is known to exist in the Cherokee language). Still others claim that the Algonquin word "awaunaguss" is the antecendent of "Yankee," or that the Indian pronunciation of "Anglais" was "Yangees." No matter its derivation, "Yankee" has come to signify a frugalness of character, directness in communication, shrewdness in business affairs, devotion to ethics, sense of responsibility, and unbounding ingenuity that the twentieth-century descendants of Irish, Italian, Polish, Russian, Portuguese, and French Canadian immigrants, and yes, the English and Scots Puritan colonists, display with continued determination.

Mount Washington Observatory (previous pages) stands on the highest peak in New England at 6,288 feet. Above: picnickers in the Maine woods enjoy watermelon at a party in August 1894.